Self-Care
ESSENTIALS®

A SIMPLE GUIDE TO MANAGING YOUR HEALTH CARE AND LIVING WELL

WELLNESS COUNCIL OF AMERICA

About **Self-Care Essentials**

Copyright & Trademark

Self-Care Essentials: A Simple Guide To Managing Your Health Care & Living Well

The information contained in this guide is based on the best health information available and has been reviewed for accuracy. This information is not intended to replace the advice of your healthcare provider. If you have any questions about managing your own health and/or seeking medical care, please contact a medical professional.

Wellness Council of America

17002 Marcy Street, Suite 140
Omaha, NE 68118
PH: (402) 827-3590 ★ FX: (402) 827-3594
www.welcoa.org

Editorial Staff

EXECUTIVE EDITOR
David Hunnicutt, PhD

Dr. Hunnicutt is President of the Wellness Council of America. As a leader in the field of health promotion, his vision has led to the creation of numerous publications designed to link health promotion objectives to business outcomes.

MEDICAL DIRECTOR
Richard Collins, MD

Dr. Collins, "The Cooking Cardiologist," is a nationally recognized expert on obesity and weight management and is known for his devotion to creating culinary dishes using only ingredients known to promote good health.

MANAGING EDITOR
Brittanie Leffelman, MS

DIRECTOR OF MARKETING
William Kizer, Jr.

DESIGN TEAM
Adam Paige, Justin Eggspuehler, Graden Hudson

Wellness Council of America [WELCOA]
17002 Marcy Street, Suite 140
Omaha, NE 68118
PH: (402) 827-3590 | FX: (402) 827-3594
www.welcoa.org

Introduction: Getting Started

Common Conditions

Common Conditions II

Relieving Aches & Pains

Chronic Conditions

Medical Consumerism

Getting Active

Managing Weight

Table of Contents

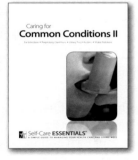

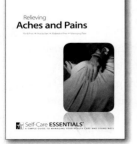

Introduction: Getting Started

Common Conditions

Common Conditions II

Relieving Aches & Pains

Chronic Conditions

Medical Consumerism

Getting Active

Managing Weight

Introduction:
Getting Started

Common
Conditions

Common
Conditions II

Relieving
Aches & Pains

Chronic
Conditions

Medical
Consumerism

Getting
Active

Managing
Weight

Self-Care **Simplicity**

The Pearl of Great Price

It has been said, "Health is not valued until sickness comes." Sadly, most people don't understand the true value of their health...until they lose it.

But it doesn't have to be this way.

Health truly is the pearl of great price, and with some care and attention, it can be protected for a lifetime.

In fact, we now know that if people pay attention to managing their health and medical care—and work in concert with their healthcare providers—it is possible to lead a long, healthy, and productive life.

And isn't that what a great life is really all about...living long and living well?

The Benefits of Good Health

Think about the last time you were hurt, sick, or just not feeling well. If you're like most people, you know that when that happens, it's hard to be at the top of your game...whether you were trying to get things done at work, taking care of things at home, or just trying to enjoy yourself in your spare time.

Plain and simple, not feeling well is a drag.

Now think about the times when you were at your best. There's a big difference between the two, don't you think? In fact, when people are in good health they're more productive, they enjoy life to the fullest, they feel good about themselves, they appreciate the company of others, and they have a much greater sense of control.

If you choose it, better health can be yours.

Practicing Self-Care

The information contained in this guide is designed to help you better manage your own health and get the most from your healthcare provider. And, if followed, the information contained in this simple guide will have you back on the road to better health almost immediately.

As you begin moving forward with the notion of better managing your own health, it's important to understand that this can best be done by working closely with your healthcare provider. In fact, developing and maintaining a meaningful and positive relationship with your healthcare provider will ensure that your health—and your family's health—is in the best hands possible.

Introducing Self-Care Essentials

This book, *Self-Care Essentials*, is a simple guide to managing your healthcare and living well. Within the following pages, you will find important information that will help you get you and your loved ones feeling better faster.

In addition to the latest information that will help you to better manage the conditions associated with not feeling well, we've included important information that will help you stay healthy for the long run.

The Simplicity of Self-Care Essentials

Managing your healthcare and living well doesn't have to be a complicated proposition. That's why we developed *Self-Care Essentials* as a guide that specifically addresses the main reasons why people seek healthcare and/or visit an emergency room in the first place. What's really amazing is that when you look at the list of why people end up in the E.R. or choose to seek healthcare, many of the reasons are potentially avoidable. And that's what this book is all about.

Common Conditions

Common Conditions II

Relieving Aches & Pains

Chronic Conditions

Medical Consumerism

Getting Active

Managing Weight

IMPORTANT!

The information contained in this book has been developed to help you better understand how to treat minor ailments and better manage certain medical conditions. The information contained in this book is not meant to replace the advice of your healthcare provider. It's important to understand that medical information changes quickly, so if you have questions or are unsure about how to handle a specific medical condition or health concern, always contact your physician, healthcare provider, or 24-hour nurse line.

Remember, your health is the pearl of great price. The information contained in this medical self-care guide can be used to increase your personal awareness of how to manage minor health issues. If you have any questions or concerns about medical issues impacting you or your family, always contact your healthcare provider.

Common Conditions

Common Conditions II

Relieving Aches & Pains

Chronic Conditions

Medical Consumerism

Getting Active

Managing Weight

Coming **To Terms**

What Self-Care ISN'T

Many people are absolutely terrified by the thought of treating themselves or making their own healthcare decisions. Understandably, our healthcare is serious business. At the same time, self-care doesn't involve performing major surgery—or surgery at all, for that matter.

Self-care also doesn't involve memorizing complex medical terms or conditions, and it doesn't involve strange home remedies, séances, or chants.

Finally, self-care isn't intended to replace the advice of your physician or healthcare provider. These individuals play an integral role on the healthcare team—and for good reason.

What Self-Care IS

If self-care isn't crystal healing or some strange home remedy, then what exactly is it?

Self-care simply means caring for yourself—it doesn't get much more straightforward than that.

In essence, self-care is all about becoming an informed healthcare consumer. It's about asking, "Do I really need to see a healthcare provider, or are there things I can do to take care of the condition myself?" It's also about prevention—taking care of yourself and your family to prevent illnesses in the first place.

At first, self-care may seem like a scary proposition. However, the following information will help you better understand the concept of self-care and how you can use it to improve your health and the health and well-being of your loved ones.

Why Is Self-Care Important?

Self-care is important simply because a big part of our medical conditions and symptoms can be treated without professional medical assistance. That's right, more times than not, we can treat ourselves in the comfort of our own homes.

Consider the following statistics—they'll shed some light on just how often we visit the healthcare provider in situations when it's actually not necessary.

Consider this…

✓ A significant portion of all healthcare visits are unnecessary.

✓ Over ⅓ of all minor medical conditions can be treated without a trip to a healthcare facility.

✓ Healthcare costs are expected to double by 2013, costing your family even more money.

Source: Larry Chapman

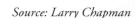

Introduction:
Getting Started

Common
Conditions

Common
Conditions II

Relieving
Aches & Pains

Chronic
Conditions

Medical
Consumerism

Getting
Active

Managing
Weight

What You Can Learn From Self-Care

By learning more about medical self-care, you'll better understand whether your health concern requires you to get professional intervention or medical attention. Again, a large number of medical conditions and ailments can be treated safely at home. Self-care will help you recognize these conditions, and help you treat them without a costly trip to your healthcare provider's office or the emergency room.

Likewise, there are situations when going to a healthcare provider is the best course of action. Self-care will help you identify these situations and help you determine how soon you should seek medical attention if it's needed.

Self-care will also help you address a number of common injuries and illnesses in your own home. In fact, *Self-Care Essentials* contains specific sections on chronic conditions and common illnesses with step-by-step instructions that will help you take charge when a minor medical situation arises.

How You Can Benefit From Self-Care

There's no denying it, healthcare costs are going up. Doctor's appointments, emergency room visits, and hospital stays aren't cheap. In fact, healthcare costs have been rising about twice as fast as peoples' incomes. In preventing unnecessary healthcare and emergency room visits, self-care has the potential of saving you money throughout the course of the year.

Additionally, self-care will help you save time. Considering travel time, time spent in the waiting room, the time you're with your provider, and your commute home, a trip to a healthcare provider or emergency room can be a time-consuming venture. But by practicing self-care you'll save time.

And don't forget that practicing self-care can also instill in you a sense of confidence, allowing you to accurately determine if, and when, professional medical assistance is needed.

Finally, practicing self-care makes you an informed consumer, allowing you to take control of your health and the health of your family. This control will help you make better health decisions—whether preventive or urgent.

Remember, practicing medical self-care need not be a daunting proposition. In fact, the more you learn about managing your own health—and working in concert with your healthcare provider—the more comfortable you'll feel with the whole process. Sure, there will be some tension associated with learning new things, but in time you can be a master when it comes to self-care.

"**Over ⅓ of all minor medical conditions** can be treated without a trip to a healthcare facility."

Information **You Can Use**

Information Is Power

As our nation's healthcare system continues to advance and evolve at a rapid pace, making confident decisions about personal and family health becomes increasingly difficult and confusing. But the fact is, it doesn't have to be. Armed with the right information, you can take command over your health and healthcare. Again, that's what this book is designed to do.

Self-Care Essentials: A Simple Guide to Managing Your Health Care and Living Well is a straightforward self-care book designed to instill a sense of empowerment when it comes to personal and family healthcare decisions. From cover to cover, you'll find the latest health information on the topics most essential to your health—and the health of your family. In the following pages, you'll learn about…

Chapter 1:
Common Conditions

Many of the common conditions we face in life aren't life threatening, or debilitating in the long run. But these common conditions are almost always discomforting and troublesome. But, by knowing how to recognize and respond to these conditions, you can speed healing and find relief. In the section entitled, *Common Conditions*, you'll learn how to conquer the cold and flu; soothe a sore throat; suppress a cough; fight a fever; as well as relieve nausea and vomiting.

Chapter 2:
Common Conditions II

In the second section on *Common Conditions*, you'll learn how to fight ear infections; relieve respiratory conditions; treat urinary tract infections; as well as how to respond to eye and vision problems.

Chapter 3:
Aches and Pains

Though aches and pains are a common part of life, we don't have to resign ourselves to suffering with them. In fact, there are a number of strategies to help prevent aches and pains from occurring—as well as speed healing when they do occur. In the section entitled, **Aches and Pains**, you'll learn how to treat back pain; find relief for headaches; deal with abdominal pain like gas or diarrhea; as well as manage pain in general.

Chapter 4:
Chronic Conditions

In an age of rapid medical advancements many chronic conditions like asthma and diabetes can now be managed—with the help of your healthcare professional—in the comfort of your own home. In fact, by employing the strategies outlined in this section, it's possible to live a relatively normal and healthy life, despite having a chronic condition. In the section entitled, **Chronic Conditions**, you'll learn some valuable strategies for managing many chronic

conditions including cholesterol; blood pressure; heart disease; diabetes; arthritis; cancer; and asthma.

Chapter 5:
Medical Consumerism

Becoming a wise medical consumer is an important step to leading a long and healthy life. A wise medical consumer is able to negotiate the healthcare system with ease, as well as maximize interactions with their healthcare team. The section on **Medical Consumerism** outlines key information on visiting your healthcare provider; understanding medical screenings; managing medications; avoiding medical errors; and utilizing health risk appraisals.

Chapter 6:
Getting Active

Most Americans get little vigorous exercise at work or during leisure hours. Today, only a few jobs still require vigorous physical activity. Evidence suggests that even low- to moderate-intensity activities can have both short- and long-term benefits. In this section, you'll learn some valuable strategies for how you can increase your physical activity and reap the benefits.

Chapter 7:
Managing Weight

According to several health experts, overweight and obesity has become the number one health problem in the United States today. The majority of Americans are either overweight or obese, and the end appears to be nowhere in sight. Part of addressing this important health issue is taking personal responsibility for your own weight. In this section, we'll outline ways to assess your weight as well as methods to help you maintain a healthy weight.

Common
Conditions

Common
Conditions II

Relieving
Aches & Pains

Chronic
Conditions

Medical
Consumerism

Getting
Active

Managing
Weight

Practicing **Self-Care Essentials**

Common
Conditions

Common
Conditions II

Relieving
Aches & Pains

Chronic
Conditions

Medical
Consumerism

Getting
Active

Managing
Weight

Practice Makes Perfect

Self-Care Essentials is an important tool at your disposal for taking care of yourself, as well as your loved ones. In fact, self-care books like *Self-Care Essentials* have improved health, saved lives, and saved countless hours and dollars spent in, and on, unnecessary healthcare and emergency room visits.

But the fact of the matter is, this book won't be very helpful if you don't know how to use it, or if it isn't handy when you need it most. The following suggestions will help you maximize the power of *Self-Care Essentials* in improving your health, and the health of your family.

Read It Before You Need It

By reading *Self-Care Essentials* now, before a medical situation arises, you'll be better prepared to respond should you need to. Start by paging through the book, looking over each of the following sections to get a handle on the information within. Next, look over the sections on conditions you're most likely to experience, or that you experience frequently. Then, look over the sections on any chronic conditions that you may be experiencing.

Then, read about the remaining conditions, should those specific situations ever arise. Lastly, read the section on Medical Consumerism to find out how you can maximize your experiences within the healthcare system itself.

Becoming a well-informed medical consumer is an important part of taking control of your health and your healthcare. *Self-Care Essentials* can help you get the job done.

In addition to just treating common and non-life threatening medical issues, *Self-Care Essentials* also helps you to prevent problems before they occur. In the last two sections of this book, we address the topics of exercise and managing weight. When practiced together, these two health behaviors can help you and your family avoid numerous health issues and increase your likelihood of living long, healthy and vibrant lives.

Keep It Where You Can Find It

Keeping your self-care book in a convenient, accessible location will help to ensure that you find the answers you need, when you need them. A good place to store your self-care book is with your first-aid kit. By storing this book with your first-aid kit, you'll have the information and the tools at hand when you need them the most. Throughout this book, different self-care techniques are discussed, and often times, these techniques require the resources of your first-aid kit. Having your self-care book and first-aid kit hand-in-hand will help you respond quickly and speed relief when faced with a medical situation.

Introduction:
Getting Started

Common
Conditions

Common
Conditions II

Relieving
Aches & Pains

Chronic
Conditions

Medical
Consumerism

Getting
Active

Managing
Weight

Step By Step

When a medical situation arises, *Self-Care Essentials* will help you make decisions about the best course of treatment for your condition. But remember, if you are ever in doubt about whether you need to seek professional medical assistance—SEEK MEDICAL ASSISTANCE OR CALL 911.

The following steps will guide you through the self-care decision-making process.

Decide whether or not to seek professional medical assistance. In many cases, the information in this book will help you to better understand when you can effectively manage a healthcare concern at home. However, there are times when it's less clear. In these instances, when you have questions or concerns, it's always wise to touch base with your healthcare provider, physician, or pharmacist.

Look up your specific condition. Each of the conditions addressed in *Self-Care Essentials* is organized in a way to help you better understand your condition and how to treat it most effectively. Once you've found your condition, refer to the specific subsections that include: About The Condition; Signs & Symptoms; When To Seek Care; Home Treatment; Frequently Asked Questions; and Prevention for more specific information about the condition you're experiencing.

Treat your condition—if appropriate. The self-care suggestions offered in the "Home Treatment" sections under each condition are designed to help you treat your specific

condition in the comfort of your own home. If you have any questions about treating your condition, contact your healthcare provider for information more specific to you. If you have any doubt about whether your condition is in need of professional medical attention, seek care immediately.

Review, Review, Review

Be sure to constantly review the information contained in *Self-Care Essentials*. The more familiar you are with the specific conditions and treatments addressed within the pages of this book, the better you will be at responding to and making confident decisions about your health, and the health of your loved ones.

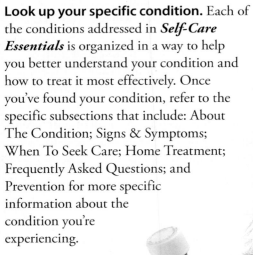

Introduction:
Getting Started

Common
Conditions

Common
Conditions II

Relieving
Aches & Pains

Chronic
Conditions

Medical
Consumerism

Getting
Active

Managing
Weight

Dancing **With Your Doctor**

Put Your Right Foot In

Interacting with your healthcare provider is a lot like dancing…and it definitely takes two to tango.

Although it sounds a little bit hokey, the image of dancing with your healthcare provider is a pretty good one. Both parties need to do their part in order for everything to work.

And, when it comes to managing your health—not to mention the health of your loved ones—the better the interaction with your healthcare provider, the better the potential outcome.

To help you interact more effectively with your healthcare provider, use these important tips.

TIP #1
Share In The Responsibility

Although this may come as a surprise, it is important to understand that your provider can't do it all—they need your help. In order to make the most out of the relationship, you must assume your fair share of the responsibility…to be a good partner, you've got to learn the right steps to take and then move in harmony with your provider.

Remember, no matter what changes or where you go, YOU are always there.

TIP #2
Keep Good Records

As you age, your medical file becomes more complex. Plan for emergencies by having a readily available personal record of your current health status, medications, and past medical history—the information contained in the rest of this book will help you do that.

Also remember to be thorough in your collection of data—it's a good bet that your medical records will be scattered throughout different healthcare systems.

The bottom line is this: keep a copy of all of your records or obtain a summary of office visits and hospitalizations. Specifically, you should always have the capability of knowing the following:

✓ Immunizations and dates

✓ A current medication list including herbs, supplements, etc.

✓ Updated family history

✓ Allergies

✓ Operations and dates

✓ Active medical illnesses

TIP #3
Know Your Numbers

Most adult Americans have had their cholesterol measured at one time, but few individuals know their total cholesterol levels or the breakdown of the good and bad cholesterol. The common response of many patients is that "my previous healthcare provider said everything was OK."

Also, it's a good thing to know your blood pressure readings and record them. Keep track of your weight and height, too. As you age, weight can slowly increase each year and height eventually will decrease. These seem like simple numbers, but these may be very important values for your present healthcare provider. With obesity, diabetes, and osteoporosis (just to mention a few) increasing at an alarming rate, it's a good idea to keep close track.

Again, always obtain a copy of your tests. You may not understand the terminology, but the results may be very useful to your current healthcare provider.

TIP #4
Practice Medical Self-Care

To get the most out of the experience, keep track of your symptoms and signs. When did they begin? How have they progressed? What symptoms are you presently experiencing?

Perhaps more importantly, what have you done to address your issues? Believe it or not, a lot of conditions can be treated by you…at home.

Again, we'll cover more of this information in other sections; still you'd be surprised how useful and effective self-care can be to you and your healthcare provider.

TIP #5
Be Honest

It sounds simple, but many times, we minimize our bad behaviors. If your healthcare provider asks about risky or sensitive behavior, be frank and truthful.

Continued on the following page…

Common Conditions

Common Conditions II

Relieving Aches & Pains

Chronic Conditions

Medical Consumerism

Getting Active

Managing Weight

11 of the 'A Guide to a Healthy Lifestyle' health promotion workb

Dancing With Your Doctor

Continued...

Common Conditions

Common Conditions II

Relieving Aches & Pains

Chronic Conditions

Medical Consumerism

Getting Active

Managing Weight

TIP #6
Engage And Enjoy

Do not feel intimidated. Instead, use your time wisely and comfortably, prioritizing your thoughts and concerns. Write down your concerns ahead of time, but do not pull out a list of 100 questions. Also, be sure to prioritize your questions.

In many respects, visiting your healthcare provider should be like taking your car in for accident repairs. Avoid the trap of bringing a long list of things that need to be done. It will only overwhelm the person who can help you most by leaving little time for major work. Work with your healthcare provider…connect… partner…and most of all…relax.

TIP #7
Be Willing To Subject Yourself To Probing And Prodding

Tests take time. Nothing is easy. Close quarters with some tests can cause uncomfortable feelings. Metal probes, rubber hoses, and latex gloves can also be a little unnerving. But do your part. Ask for help or alternatives if you are really concerned. You'd be surprised, most medical staff will work hard to help to ease any discomfort.

TIP #8
Take Notes

Healthcare providers sometimes forget that they talk in strange terms. Ask for clarification if a term is not familiar. Medications often have long unfamiliar names, both generic and trade names. Diagnoses appear to be written in foreign languages. Ask for the proper spelling and meaning. Healthcare providers often abbreviate words and most medical records seem confusing. Take notes, ask questions, and get clarification.

Introduction:
Getting Started

Common
Conditions

Common
Conditions II

Relieving
Aches & Pains

Chronic
Conditions

Medical
Consumerism

Getting
Active

Managing
Weight

TIP #9
Get To Know The Office Staff... Jot Down Names

Some of the most important medical office allies you'll ever have are the office staff. Get to know the front office, the scheduling secretary, nurses, and billing representatives. These individuals are the key to your satisfaction with your healthcare provider. Establish a meaningful relationship with these folks and you are a step ahead of the game.

TIP #10
Follow Through

Oftentimes, people will go to great lengths to feel better fast. But here's a strange thing...just when they find relief, they discard all of the information previously given to them. If you want to dance well with your healthcare provider, follow through on their recommendations—even after you start to feel better.

Learning More

Knowledge is key during the decision making process. The more you know about health problems, how to take care of health problems, and the healthcare delivery system, the more confident you will be that the choices you make are going to be safe and effective.

There are a number of resources at your disposal to help you become self-care savvy. Some possible resources include...

▶ **Medically sound self-care books.** A variety of reputable organizations publish self-care texts that walk you through treatment options step-by-step.

▶ **Healthcare providers.** Don't be afraid to contact your healthcare provider to ask questions and determine a course of treatment that's appropriate.

▶ **Non-profit health organizations.** The American Cancer Society and the American Heart Association are excellent resources you can use to learn more about your health and well-being.

▶ **Health related websites.** The rapid growth of Internet technology has given us instant access to a wealth of health information—some good, some bad. Reliable websites like WebMD can be utilized to educate yourself on salient health topics.

▶ **Government publications.** Government organizations often publish reports on common health conditions. These reports are helpful, and can be easily accessed online.

In Summary

Your healthcare relationship is a dance between you and the provider. Each has a responsibility. Knowing this relationship will give you and your doctor the best opportunity to maintain your health.

Caring for
Common Conditions

Colds & Flu ★ Sore Throat ★ Coughs ★ Fighting Fever ★ Nausea & Vomiting

Self-Care **ESSENTIALS**®
A SIMPLE GUIDE TO MANAGING YOUR HEALTH CARE AND LIVING WELL

Introduction: Getting Started

Common Conditions

Common Conditions II

Relieving Aches & Pains

Chronic Conditions

Medical Consumerism

Getting Active

Managing Weight

Understanding **Colds & Flu**

About Colds & Flu

With all the medical advances we witness every day, it's disappointing that we still haven't figured out how to defeat the common cold and flu. These maladies have been with humanity at least since written history began. The average American will suffer through two to four colds each year, and millions will also endure at least one bout of the flu. Each episode can represent a week or two of lost productivity and enjoyment.

Even though there is no cure, there are things you can do to reduce your chances of catching one of these nasty conditions. And if you do catch a cold or flu, there are self-care techniques you can employ to ease your misery and feel better fast.

Signs & Symptoms

One of the first things you'll need to determine to get on the road to recovery is whether you have a cold or the flu. Although they can feel similar, cold and flu are very different illnesses.

Is it a Cold or the Flu?

Both colds and flu are caused by viruses, and both share the symptoms of fatigue, cough, and nasal congestion. Colds, however, are restricted to the nose, throat, and surrounding air passages. Most colds are not accompanied by fever, chills, or the more severe symptoms identified with flu, and recovery is faster. Flu is almost always more severe than a cold. It hits suddenly with aches, a high fever, and chills. The flu typically runs its course in about a week, although you may feel uncomfortable for several weeks.

Symptom	Cold	Flu
Fever	low-grade (up to 102°)	102-104°+, 3-4 days
Headache	rare	prominent, sudden onset
General aches	slight	usual, often severe
Fatigue or weakness	mild	can last 2-3 weeks
Extreme exhaustion	never	early and prominent
Stuffy nose	common	sometimes
Sneezing	usual	sometimes
Sore throat	common	sometimes
Chest discomfort, cough	mild to moderate	common, can become severe

"Approximately **four**

the flu are reported

Introduction:
Getting Started

**Common
Conditions**

Common
Conditions II

Relieving
Aches & Pains

Chronic
Conditions

Medical
Consumerism

Getting
Active

Managing
Weight

✚ A Self-Care Essential

Find a Flu Shot. There are several "flu shot locators" available online. These mini search tools will help you find a flu shot clinic near you. Type "flu shot locator" into a search engine to access a reputable site—the American Lung Association is usually a good bet (***lungusa.org***). These locators are usually most active during the months of October and November of each year.

When To Seek Care

The symptoms described here can be signs of a condition much more serious than an average cold or flu. See your healthcare professional if you're experiencing any of the following.

⚕ If your symptoms last for more than 10 days.

⚕ If the pain or swelling over your sinuses gets worse when you bend over or move your head, especially with a fever of 101°F or higher.

⚕ If your cold is accompanied by trouble breathing or wheezing.

⚕ If you experience swollen, painful neck glands or pain in the ears.

⚕ A headache that persists during a cold or flu is a sign that you should see a healthcare provider.

⚕ If you have a sore throat that is very red or has white spots.

⚕ A cough with phlegm that is green, gray, or yellow means you may need to see a healthcare provider.

⚕ Seek medical care if a temperature is higher than 102°F in a 3-month to 3-year-old child; over 104°F in a 3 to 64-year-old; or 102°F or higher in someone age 65 or older.

⚕ If a foul smell comes from the throat, nose, or ears.

Home Treatment

Check out the following tips to feel better fast when you are battling a cold or flu.

⌂ **Drink Fluids**—drinking at least eight, 8 oz. glasses of fluid daily thins your mucus, helping it to flow. Hot drinks and soups are especially effective.

⌂ **Humidify Your Environment**—moisture helps. Use the shower, a humidifier, or breathe over a bowl of hot water.

⌂ **Get Rest**—going to work with a cold isn't necessarily going to make it worse, but keep in mind you are most contagious in the first 48 hours.

⌂ **Cough and Blow**—blow your nose gently and often, and cough as needed. You want to keep the phlegm moving, not suppress it.

⌂ **Gargle**—gargle three times daily with salt water to soothe your sore throat. Salt helps sterilize the bacteria in the back of your throat and promotes the healing of inflamed tissues. To make a salt solution, stir ½ teaspoon of salt in a glass of warm water and gargle for 30-60 seconds.

⌂ **Don't Take Antibiotics**—unless there's solid medical evidence that you have a secondary bacterial infection. If you are unsure, see your healthcare provider.

⌂ **Take an Over-The-Counter (OTC) Remedy**— Take single-ingredient products like Sudafed or Robitussin only as needed and as directed. Make sure you read the label warnings and only take something if you really need it. Be careful about interactions between over-the-counter and prescribed medications.

Continued on the following page...

ion severe cases of
h year worldwide."

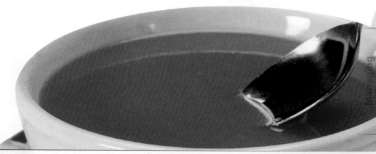

Understanding **Colds & Flu**

Continued...

Introduction: Getting Started

Common Conditions

Common Conditions II

Relieving Aches & Pains

Chronic Conditions

Medical Consumerism

Getting Active

Managing Weight

Meningitis

Meningitis is an infection of the tissues and fluid surrounding the brain and spinal cord. Because meningitis can range from mild to life threatening—and because it can mimic the symptoms of the common cold and flu, especially in children—it's important to be aware of the specific symptoms of meningitis.

Symptoms of Meningitis

✓ Confusion and decreased level of consciousness

✓ Seizures   ✓ Vomiting

✓ Sensitivity to light   ✓ Skin rash

✓ Fatigue   ✓ Dizziness

✓ Muscle aches and weakness

✓ Stiff neck

✓ Loss of appetite

✓ In babies, symptoms may also include fever, irritability, decreased appetite, rash, and a shrill cry.

✓ Young children with meningitis may act like they have the flu, cough, or have trouble breathing.

✓ Older adults and those with depressed immune systems may have only a mild headache and fever.

If these symptoms are present—especially in children—see your healthcare provider right away. Often, meningitis caused by a virus can be treated simply at home because symptoms typically disappear within two weeks. Meningitis caused by bacteria, on the other hand, needs to be treated with antibiotics, and can be deadly if not properly cared for.

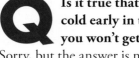
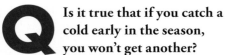

Frequently Asked Questions

With all the myths floating around about colds and flu, it helps to be able to separate fact from fiction. Take a look at the following frequently asked questions (FAQs)—they'll help you put ineffective remedies to rest and speed recovery.

Q **Will antibiotics help me recover faster?**
No. Antibiotics work only against bacterial infections. They're useless for colds and flu, which are viral infections. But they may be needed for any secondary bacterial infections that may develop as complications of your cold or flu, like an ear or sinus infection.

Q **Is it good to take a cough suppressant whenever you have a cough?**
Not necessarily. If your cough is productive (meaning phlegm is coming up from your lungs), coughing can help you get better faster. Remember, if you are coughing up phlegm that is green, gray, or yellow, contact your healthcare provider. A dry, nonproductive cough that keeps you from sleeping has no benefit. Try a single-ingredient cough suppressant containing dextromethorphan at night.

Q **Does taking Vitamin C help a cold?**
Some researchers believe so. Vitamin C intake can possibly shorten the length of a cold and even make it less severe. However, it's most effective when taken in the early stages of the virus. Try oranges or orange juice, strawberries, and/or supplements. (Always follow the recommended dosage).

Q **Is it true that if you catch a cold early in the season, you won't get another?**
Sorry, but the answer is no. There are hundreds of different cold viruses. You won't catch the same one again, but you may catch another.

Introduction: Getting Started

Common Conditions

Common Conditions II

Relieving Aches & Pains

Chronic Conditions

Medical Consumerism

Getting Active

Managing Weight

Prevention

There's no question about it—the best way to deal with a cold or flu is to avoid it in the first place. By taking a few precautions, you can dramatically cut your chances of picking up one of these viruses, and be well on your way to staying healthy and productive this cold and flu season. Here are some tips to consider.

 Wash your hands before you touch your face or eat, after using the bathroom, and after touching shared items like telephones or computers. Use antibacterial soap, lather well, and use warm water. Washing your hands often may be the single most important thing you can do to avoid a cold or flu.

 Get at least eight hours of sleep each night so your body isn't run down.

 Avoid physical contact with sick people if possible.

 Consider staying home during the first few days of a cold, when you're most contagious. Wash your hands after contact with sick people.

 Eat a healthy, vitamin-rich diet, including five servings of fruits and vegetables daily.

 Use a humidifier during cold and flu season—dry nasal passages are less resistant to viruses.

 Use disposable tissues instead of cloth handkerchiefs to reduce germs.

 Nurture your relationships with friends, family, and your community. A large circle of friends is associated with better resistance to illness.

 Don't share towels, eating utensils, or toothbrushes.

 Consider getting a flu shot.

A Shot of Prevention

An annual flu shot is a way to reduce your chances of getting the flu. Influenza is a serious condition, and no matter what your age, you can still get it. The flu causes 50,000 deaths each year (mostly among those aged 65 years or older) and 114,000 hospitalizations in the U.S. alone.

Much of the illness and death caused by the flu can be prevented by yearly flu shots. People in certain "high-risk" groups (those who may develop serious complications from the flu), and people who are in close contact with those at high-risk, should get a flu shot every year.

Who Should Get A Flu Shot?

✓ Persons over the age of 50.

✓ A child age 6 months to 4 years.

✓ Those living in long-term care facilities.

✓ Those who are pregnant.

✓ People with chronic conditions and/or those whose immune system is weakened.

✓ Anybody in close contact with people at high-risk for getting a serious case of the flu.

Is A Flu Shot Right For You?

Some people should talk with a healthcare provider before getting a flu shot. These people include:

✓ Those who have had a severe allergic reaction to hen eggs or to a previous flu shot.

✓ Individuals who have a history of Guillain-Barré Syndrome (GBS).

✓ Those who presently have a fever.

Get a flu shot six to eight weeks before flu season begins (sometime in October or November). According to the NIH, getting a shot at this time will give your body time to produce enough antibodies to mount a strong defense during flu season, which hits its stride between late December and early March. Remember to get a new vaccine every year. Vaccines are designed for specific strains of the flu, which can be different every year.

Vitamin C is most effective when **taken before illness strikes or immediately after** you've been exposed to a cold or the flu.

Understanding **Sore Throats**

About Sore Throats

Sore throats can be one of the most annoying and uncomfortable ailments you can have. It's difficult to speak, swallow, or get a good night's sleep. The good news is, sore throats are usually the result of a minor illness, and with proper care and attention, can often be treated quickly and effectively at home.

Types of Sore Throat

In this section we'll discuss two of the most typical kinds of sore throat—the common, mild sore throat often associated with other illnesses or environmental factors, and strep throat, which is caused by a more serious bacterial infection.

Common Sore Throat. Most often you'll find that the common sore throat accompanies the cold or flu. Postnasal drip (nasal drainage down the back of the throat) is usually the culprit. The common sore throat can also be caused by smoking, air pollution, low humidity, yelling, or breathing through the mouth for long periods of time.

Strep Throat. Strep throat is caused by a streptococcal (strep) bacterial infection in the back of the throat. Strep throat accounts for about 10 percent of sore throats in adults and between 15 and 30 percent of sore throats in children. Strep throat hits quickly and painfully, causing a sudden and severe sore throat. Strep throat is highly contagious, and is most often passed to others when an infected person expels strep bacteria by coughing or sneezing.

Signs & Symptoms

Common Sore Throat or Strep?

Now that we know more about common sore throats and strep bacterial infections, it's important to be able to distinguish which type of sore throat you are experiencing. Check out the symptoms for both the common sore throat and strep bacterial infection listed below. In most cases, both conditions, when recognized early, can be treated at home without a trip to your healthcare provider.

Symptoms of A Common Sore Throat

✓ A dry, scratchy throat

✓ Pain or irritation in the throat, especially when swallowing or speaking

✓ Coughing and sneezing

✓ Occasional, mild fever

✓ Runny nose and/or postnasal drip

Symptoms of Strep Throat

✓ A sudden, severe sore throat

✓ Difficulty swallowing

✓ Yellow, or white spots in the back of the throat

✓ Swollen lymph nodes and tonsils

✓ A fever of 101°F or higher

✓ A relative absence of coughing, sneezing, and stuffy nose (these symptoms are most commonly associated with a common sore throat or cold, not strep throat)

*"Gargling **every hour** with a warm salt water solution can help soothe your sore throat."*

Introduction: Getting Started

Common Conditions

Common Conditions II

Relieving Aches & Pains

Chronic Conditions

Medical Consumerism

Getting Active

Managing Weight

Introduction:
Getting Started

**Common
Conditions**

Common
Conditions II

Relieving
Aches & Pains

Chronic
Conditions

Medical
Consumerism

Getting
Active

Managing
Weight

A Self-Care Essential

Soothe Your Sore Throat. Gargling with a salt water solution can ease your sore throat. Here's how to do it:

▶ Stir ½ tsp. of salt in an 8 oz. glass of warm water

▶ Gargle for 30-60 seconds

▶ Repeat as needed

When To Seek Care

If you are experiencing persistent and severe symptoms, they could be the sign of a much more serious condition. The following symptoms indicate you may need to seek professional medical help for your sore throat.

⚕ Seek medical help if you are drooling or having difficulty breathing or swallowing.

⚕ If you have a sore throat without a cold or runny nose.

⚕ If you have joint pain.

⚕ If you have a stiff neck, and severe headache.

⚕ If you have tender, swollen lymph glands.

⚕ If your voice is muffled or you're having difficulty speaking.

⚕ See a medical provider if you develop a skin rash.

⚕ If you have a fever of more than 101°F (103°F for children) or a fever that lasts for more than two days.

⚕ If you experience a sore throat (or mouth ulcers) lasting more than a couple of days.

If your doctor suspects that you have strep throat, a throat culture or rapid strep test—simple tests to determine the cause of your sore throat—will be ordered. In most cases, you'll learn the results of the test within an hour or two. If you test positive for strep, your doctor will most likely prescribe an antibiotic to help you feel better.

! **Key Point:** In some cases strep throat can trigger rheumatic fever, a condition that affects the heart and joints. Symptoms include weakness, joint pain, and jerking movements in the arms and legs, among others. See a healthcare professional if you experience these symptoms.

Continued on the following page...

Cold Sores

Cold sores, also known as fever blisters, are small, red blisters, which form on the inside or outside of a person's mouth, typically on the lip. Caused by a herpes virus, cold sores often appear after a cold, fever, or prolonged sun exposure, and are also associated with stress. A painful proposition, cold sores require patience because they take anywhere from seven to 10 days to fully heal.

If you're experiencing a cold sore, the following steps may help you find relief and speed healing.

✓ Apply ice to the cold sore three times per day to reduce swelling.

✓ Use petroleum jelly or other products designed to soothe and protect cold sores.

✓ Use an over-the-counter product containing vitamin E or aloe vera to help reduce pain.

Despite the fact that cold sores are commonplace for the majority of Americans, there are several steps you can take to prevent cold sores. To reduce your chances of experiencing a cold sore, put the following tips into practice.

✓ Use sunscreen or ChapStick to shield your lips from being exposed to harmful UV light.

✓ Avoid close contact with someone who has or recently had a cold sore.

✓ Find ways to reduce stress in your life.

While most cold sores are painful, they're seldom the sign of a serious problem. If your cold sore lasts longer than 2 weeks, or if you have multiple cold sores in a short amount of time, talk with your healthcare provider. He or she may prescribe a medication to reduce the severity and frequency of your cold sores.

A Word of Caution: If you have a cold sore, avoid touching the sore, and keep your hands away from your eyes. Herpes virus infections may have potentially serious complications, especially if they spread to the eyes. In fact, this is a frequent cause of corneal blindness in the U.S. If you're experiencing a burning pain in or a rash near the eye or on the tip of your nose, see your healthcare provider immediately.

Understanding **Sore Throats**
Continued...

Home Treatment

As mentioned before, in the majority of cases, common sore throat and strep throat can be treated at home. Use the tips mentioned here to treat yourself for sore throat or strep throat and feel better fast.

Common Sore Throat

⌂ **Drink eight, 8 oz. glasses of fluids daily** to help soothe your throat.

⌂ **Gargle every hour with warm salt water to reduce discomfort and swelling.** To make a salt solution, stir ½ teaspoon of salt in a glass of warm water and gargle for 30-60 seconds.

⌂ **Try over-the-counter throat lozenges and cough drops** to soothe a sore throat.

⌂ **Use a decongestant** to help relieve postnasal drip.

⌂ **Rest your voice.**

⌂ **Take over-the-counter pain relievers** (like ibuprofen or acetaminophen). Do not give aspirin to children.

⌂ **Use a humidifier** to keep nasal passages moist and more resistant to viruses.

Strep Throat

Treatment for strep throat is very similar to the treatment of a common sore throat. With this in mind, try the following tips.

⌂ **Eat and drink cold foods and liquids** to soothe your throat.

⌂ **Drink extra fluids** in addition to the usual eight, 8 oz. glasses—fluids help flush the system and speed healing.

⌂ **Get plenty of rest** (at least 8 to 10 hours nightly).

Note: Even though strep throat can be treated at home, doctor prescribed antibiotics are the most common option. These antibiotics may relieve discomfort and shorten the time a person is contagious.

Frequently Asked Questions

Take a look at the following frequently asked questions—they'll help you further understand this condition, and better care for yourself and your family.

Q **I've had a sore throat for a while now, could it be mono?**
Infectious mononucleosis (mono), often known as "the kissing disease," includes sore throat as one of its symptoms. Mono is very common among the U.S. population, but just because you have a sore throat, it doesn't mean you have mono. If your symptoms last for more than a week or two, it may be a good idea to contact your healthcare professional.

Q **What increases the risk for strep throat?**
Plain and simple, increased risk for strep throat revolves around your close contact with others who are infected. Coughing, sneezing, and touching others who have the infection can spread strep.

Q **Who is affected by strep throat?**
Strep throat is responsible for 5 to 15 percent of sore throats in adults, and up to 30 percent of sore throats in children. Strep throat is most commonly found in children between the ages of 3 and 15.

Side tabs: Introduction: Getting Started · Common Conditions · Common Conditions II · Relieving Aches & Pains · Chronic Conditions · Medical Consumerism · Getting Active · Managing Weight

Q **I thought sore throats and strep throat were caused by cold weather. Isn't that true?**

No, it's not true. Common sore throats are often the result of a cold or the flu, and strep throat is a bacterial infection. Sore throat is more common during colder months simply because individuals spend more time indoors around each other, and tend to spread illnesses more easily.

Q **I've heard that strep throat can lead to other complications. Is this true?**

Strep throat can lead to other infections—like rheumatic fever—but only in rare cases. If your strep throat is severe and not treated properly, it is also possible for infection to spread into the middle ear or sinuses.

Prevention

Though there is very little we can do to prevent a sore throat or strep throat altogether, there are, however, a number of powerful steps we can take to lessen the chances of developing one of these conditions. Practicing the following steps can help you avoid the pain and discomfort associated with a sore or strep throat.

 Avoid contact with anyone you know who has strep throat.

 Wash your hands and face often (hands should be lathered well with antibacterial soap and warm water).

 Don't share eating and drinking utensils.

 Humidify your home (humidity keeps mucus membranes more resistant to bacteria).

 Drink at least eight, 8 oz. glasses of fluids daily.

 Identify and avoid irritants such as smoke or yelling that cause sore throats.

About "Mono" (Mononucleosis)

Sore throats are often associated with and confused for a condition known as Mononucleosis, A.K.A "the kissing disease." Mononucleosis (or mono) is a viral infection common in older teens and adolescents. Its symptoms, in addition to a sore throat, include persistent fatigue, weakness, vertigo, swollen lymph nodes, aches, and an enlarged spleen. It is common for mono to last several weeks, but it is typically not severe. The best treatment for mono is getting plenty of rest, proper hydration, and taking over-the-counter medications to relieve general aches. You'll want to work with your healthcare provider to identify and treat mono.

Is It Strep or Tonsillitis?

Strep or Tonsillitis?

Strep throat and tonsillitis share many of the same symptoms including:

✓ Red and inflamed throat with spots
✓ Fever
✓ Sore throat

The main difference between strep throat and tonsillitis is that strep throat is caused by a bacterial infection and tonsillitis is usually caused by a virus. Tonsillitis is most common in children.

Treatment

If you suspect that you have tonsillitis, you can treat symptoms with saltwater gargles, throat lozenges, and over-the-counter pain relievers. More rare cases of tonsillitis caused by bacteria may be treated like strep throat.

What About A Tonsillectomy?

Tonsillectomy, although still fairly common, isn't performed as often as it used to be. Surgery is only recommended when a chronic bacterial infection is resistant to treatment with medication, or when the infection results in serious complications.

Introduction Getting Started

Common Conditions

Common Conditions II

Relieving Aches & Pains

Chronic Conditions

Medical Consumerism

Getting Active

Managing Weight

Understanding **Coughs**

Introduction:
Getting Started

Common
Conditions

Common
Conditions II

Relieving
Aches & Pains

Chronic Conditions

Medical Consumerism

Getting Active

Managing Weight

About Coughs

Coughing is the body's natural way of protecting the lungs from irritants. A certain amount of coughing is ordinary, and even natural, and can help you breathe better. However, prolonged and violent coughing can indicate that some kind of irritant is present in your breathing passages.

Coughing can also often be a symptom of an upper respiratory viral infection like a cold or the flu. Excess mucus draining down the back of your throat (postnasal drip) is often the cause of a cough. A persistent cough is not only uncomfortable, but can also cause your voice to become raw and horse, making it difficult to speak.

Signs & Symptoms

Coughs come in two varieties: productive and nonproductive.

Productive coughs are the types that produce phlegm and mucus. Coughs of this type are healthy because they help to clear phlegm and mucus from the lungs.

Nonproductive coughs do not produce phlegm or mucus and are frequently the result of irritants such as smoke or dust. Oftentimes, nonproductive coughs occur near the end of a viral infection such as a cold.

There are many causes for both productive and nonproductive coughs.

When To Seek Care

Sometimes, a persistent, harsh cough may be an important indicator that you're experiencing a more serious medical condition. If you experience any of the following symptoms, contact your healthcare provider right away.

⚕ If you have a fever of 102°F or higher that persists.

⚕ If you become short of breath or if breathing is troubled or rapid.

⚕ If bloody, yellow, or green sputum is coughed up from the lungs.

⚕ Coughs that linger longer than a week to 10 days, (especially when other symptoms have passed) should be assessed by a healthcare professional.

"It's been estimated t
not wash their hands

Introduction:
Getting Started

Common
Conditions

Common
Conditions II

Relieving
Aches & Pains

Chronic
Conditions

Medical
Consumerism

Getting
Active

Managing
Weight

✚ A Self-Care Essential

Humidify Your Environment.
A good humidifier is worth the investment when you're sick because it will help moisturize your mucus membranes and keep you more resistant to illness. Make sure to change the filter on your humidifier as recommended—dirty filters can spread bacteria.

Home Treatment

Most coughs that people experience—though frequently uncomfortable and certainly annoying—are not the sign of a more serious condition. These coughs are easily treated and soothed by employing self-care techniques. If you're bothered by a particular cough, employing the strategies listed here may help you find the relief you're looking for.

⌂ **Drink plenty of fluids.** Drinking at least eight, 8 oz. glasses of fluid each day will help to keep your throat clear.

⌂ **Use over-the-counter cough suppressants.** Cough suppressants will help soothe your cough.

⌂ **Use medications (expectorants) to help clear your throat.** Such medications will help to increase the flow of fluids in your throat.

⌂ **Use cough drops or lozenges to help soothe an irritated throat.** These items can help to soothe a dry, scratchy, and sore throat.

⌂ **Humidify your environment.** Using a humidifier is good on your throat, makes it easier to breathe, and keeps mucus membranes more resistant to illness.

An Ounce of Prevention

Most experts agree that frequent hand washing is the best way to prevent the spread of disease. Unfortunately, it's been estimated that one out of three people do not wash their hands after using the restroom. By frequently washing your hands, you wash away germs that you have picked up from other people, contaminated surfaces, or from pets.

In addition to frequently washing your hands, there are several other techniques you should follow to help prevent the spread of disease. These include:

✓ Using a disposable tissue or handkerchief when coughing or sneezing

✓ Using a hand disinfectant such as Purell after coughing or sneezing

✓ Avoiding close contact such as shaking hands with infected persons

✓ Avoiding public restrooms

✓ Not sharing food, or eating and drinking utensils

By practicing the above behaviors, you'll better ensure your health, and the health of those around you.

1 out of 3 people do
er using the restroom."

Fighting **Fever**

Introduction:
Getting Started

Common
Conditions

Common
Conditions II

Relieving
Aches & Pains

Chronic
Conditions

Medical
Consumerism

Getting
Active

Managing
Weight

About Fevers

Simply stated, a fever is a higher than normal body temperature. Normal body temperature is, on average, 98.6°F, although body temperature from person to person can vary by as much as one degree. Additionally, your own body temperature will fluctuate throughout the day—being cooler in the morning, and rising throughout the course of the day.

Fever is not an illness, but rather a sign that your body may be fighting off a virus or bacterial infection such as a cold, urinary tract infection, mumps, measles, or chicken pox. A fever up to 101°F can be helpful in the battle because it helps the body react to an infection.

Signs & Symptoms

There are no real symptoms of fevers other than the abnormally high body temperature that is the fever itself. There are however, several different grades of fevers, some more serious than others.

Fever Grade Temperature Range	
Normal Range	97.5°F to 99.6°F
Self-Care Range	99.6°F to 102°F
Cautionary Range	102°F to 104°F
Emergency Range	104°F or higher

Although there are no real symptoms, an individual with a fever may look pale, shiver, or even have goose bumps. It is not uncommon for children to curl up in a ball to conserve body heat. No matter how cold an individual may appear, it's not a good idea to bundle them up with extra blankets or extra clothing. Doing so will only cause body temperature to further rise.

When To Seek Care

A fever of 104°F or higher that lasts longer than 2 hours is a sign that you may be experiencing a serious medical condition. You should seek medical attention if this is the case, or if you experience any of the following symptoms.

- If your fever has been more than 103°F or if you've had a fever for more than three days

- If a baby younger than three months, has a temperature of 100.5°F or higher

- If you have a fever accompanied by a severe, throbbing headache

- If you have a fever accompanied by sensitivity to light or sound

- If stiffness or pain in the neck when bending over accompanies your fever

- If the fever brings about mental confusion

- Swelling in the throat along with a fever should be evaluated by a medical professional

- See a doctor if you have a fever and are vomiting regularly

- If your fever is accompanied by breathing problems

- If your fever is accompanied by severe irritability

"A fever of **104°F or higher for longer tha**
2 hours, should be considered an emergen
Call your healthcare provider to seek advic

A Self-Care Essential

Avoid Ice and Alcohol Baths. Although ice and alcohol baths were once recommended as a means to reduce a severe fever, they can actually be counterproductive.

Home Treatment

Treating a fever may be one of the most common self-care practices you'll ever undertake, so it's good to know some keys to reducing fever and helping you or your loved one feel better as quickly as possible. Check out some general home-treatment tips for fever. In addition to these general tips, treatment tips for fevers of different grades are also listed here.

General Fever Treatment

⌂ **Drink plenty of fluids.** As your temperature begins to rise, your body uses more water. Try to get at least eight, 8 oz. glasses of water daily.

⌂ **Get plenty of rest.** Rest will help your body heal. When sick, aim for eight to 10 hours of sleep nightly.

⌂ **Eat light foods.** Your body burns more calories during a fever. Easily digested foods (like chicken broth) are best.

⌂ **Dress lightly.** Excessive clothing can further increase body temperature.

⌂ **Try taking a bath or shower with luke-warm water.** Luke-warm water can help reduce fever. Avoid cold water.

Self-Care For Specific Fever Ranges
— SELF-CARE RANGE: 99.6°F–102°F —

➤ In most cases, it is not necessary to use over-the-counter medications like acetaminophen or ibuprofen for a new fever in this range.

➤ Monitor the fever every 30 minutes.

➤ Wear cool, comfortable clothing.

Fever Related Seizures In Children

An unexplained high fever in a child can be more problematic than in an adult because of the risk of seizure. Although fever-related seizures can look dramatic and are frightening for both parent and child, they can be managed effectively. Seizures usually cause no permanent damage.

Roughly one in 20 children under the age of four will experience a fever-related seizure. Seizures usually last less than 10 minutes, and oftentimes are over in a matter of seconds. If your child is having a fever-related seizure, keep the following in mind.

✓ Lay the child on his or her side.

✓ Provide comfort by holding and reassuring the child.

✓ Do not place anything in the child's mouth to try and stop the seizure.

If your child experiences a seizure seek medical attention. If you have questions, or need help, contact your healthcare provider or nurseline.

— CAUTIONARY RANGE: 102°F–104°F —

➤ Use over-the-counter medications like acetaminophen or ibuprofen to lower the fever. (Always follow label directions). Adults may use aspirin—do not give aspirin to children!

➤ You way want to contact a healthcare professional for a fever in this range.

➤ Monitor the fever every 30 minutes.

— EMERGENCY RANGE: 104°F+ —

➤ Call your healthcare provider to seek advice; it is time to seek professional medical care at this point.

➤ Use over-the-counter medications like acetaminophen or ibuprofen to lower the fever. (Always follow label directions). Do not give aspirin to children.

➤ You may try a sponge bath of luke-warm water to reduce the fever.

➤ Monitor the fever every 30 minutes. If a fever in this range persists longer than 2 hours, you should seek medical attention immediately.

Intro Get

Common Conditions

Common Conditions II

Relieving Aches & Pains

Chronic Conditions

Medical Consumerism

Getting Active

Managing Weight

Introduction:
Getting Started

Common
Conditions

Common
Conditions II

Relieving
Aches & Pains

Chronic
Conditions

Medical
Consumerism

Getting
Active

Managing
Weight

Treating **Nausea & Vomiting**

About Nausea & Vomiting

Two uncomfortable feelings in life are nausea and vomiting. Nausea is an unpleasant, churning sensation felt down inside the stomach, whereas vomiting is the expulsion of stomach contents through the esophagus and out of the mouth. Oftentimes, vomiting is preceded and even caused by an intense feeling of nausea.

Vomiting and nausea, though not diseases in and of themselves, often indicate the presence of a common viral infection—known as gastroenteritis—in the intestines. Other causes of nausea and vomiting may include adverse reactions to certain medications, food poisoning, pregnancy, and motion sickness.

If not cared for properly, nausea and vomiting can lead to other complications that include dehydration (lack of water in the body), aspiration (food lodged in the windpipe), or even serious damage to your body including tearing the food pipe. The rest of this section is dedicated to helping you treat and manage bouts of nausea and vomiting.

Signs & Symptoms

The signs and symptoms of nausea and vomiting are easy to identify. Often a nauseated person will feel the following symptoms.

✓ Fatigue

✓ A warm or sweaty feeling

✓ Excessive saliva in the mouth

While nausea and vomiting are usually symptoms of other medical conditions, there are a number of triggers that can make a person feel nauseous or vomit.

Common Causes of Nausea & Vomiting

✓ Gastroenteritis (a common viral condition passed easily from person to person)

✓ Adverse reactions to medications

✓ Excessive consumption of alcohol

✓ Colds and flu   ✓ Food poisoning

✓ Overeating   ✓ Motion sickness

✓ Bad smells   ✓ Migraine headaches

When To Seek Care

Even though nausea and vomiting are usually not serious, sometimes a trip to the doctor may be necessary. Seek medical attention immediately in the following situations.

⚕ If you notice blood in the vomit. Blood may sometimes look like coffee grounds when partially digested.

⚕ If you get dehydrated (signs of dehydration include dry mouth, sticky saliva, and dark, yellow urine).

⚕ If you develop a stiff neck.

⚕ If you experience any chest pain.

⚕ If you have been vomiting for more than a few days and/or symptoms are becoming more frequent and severe.

Introduction:
Getting Started

**Common
Conditions**

Common
Conditions II

Relieving
Aches & Pains

Chronic
Conditions

Medical
Consumerism

Getting
Active

Managing
Weight

A Self-Care Essential

Try Sugared Soda in Moderation. A small amount of regular (not diet or sugar free) soda may help quickly soothe nausea and vomiting. Give it a try—you can find soda anywhere, and it may bring quick relief when you need it most.

Home Treatment

Treating nausea and vomiting in your home can be simple and effective. The following remedies can help calm your stomach, and help you feel better quickly.

⌂ **Refrain from eating or drinking for several hours.** (You may attempt to eat small amounts of bland food like dry toast, water, crackers and rice).

⌂ **Drink cool, clear fluids** to prevent dehydration.

⌂ **Avoid fatty, fried, or spicy foods as well as dairy items.** Also avoid alcohol, nicotine, and caffeine.

⌂ **Drink small amounts of sugared soda** (sugar helps calm the stomach).

Food Poisoning

Food poisoning is one of the most common causes of nausea and vomiting. In fact, the more than 250 existing foodborne diseases account for an estimated 76 million illnesses, 325,000 hospitalizations, and 5,200 deaths in the United States each year.

The symptoms of food poisoning often include nausea, vomiting, diarrhea, and stomach pain.

Following simple guidelines on food preparation, handling, and storage can easily prevent the vast majority of foodborne illness. The following guidelines can help you avoid the nausea and vomiting associated with many foodborne illnesses.

✓ Keep foods hot or cold—room temperature is where many bacteria grow.

✓ Set your refrigerator between 34°F and 40°F. According to the FDA, 23 percent of household refrigerators are not cold enough.

✓ Defrost meats in the refrigerator or microwave.

✓ Cook hamburger/ground meats thoroughly.

✓ Don't eat undercooked or raw eggs.

✓ Keep all cutting boards clean.

Treating Diarrhea

Diarrhea occurs when bowel movements are looser or more watery than normal. Diarrhea can be caused by a number of things including stomach flu, medications, food poisoning, or parasitic infection—just to name a few.

Thankfully, treating diarrhea is straightforward in most cases. Treatment involves the following.

Stay hydrated. Make sure to take small, frequent drinks of water several times a day. If possible, it is recommended that you drink at least one liter of water each hour.

Eat mild foods. Try the B.R.A.T diet. Bananas, rice, applesauce, and toast can be easily digested, and are used by many hospitals to control diarrhea. Avoid fatty foods, coffee, and milk products until your diarrhea subsides.

Consider OTCs. Over-the-counter medications such as Pepto-Bismol or Imodium may slow diarrhea, however, they won't speed recovery. Work with your healthcare provider to determine what's right for you.

DO YOU KNOW HOW TO CARE FOR...

Common Conditions?

Take The Self-Care Quiz

The quiz below is designed to test your knowledge on the information presented in this section. Use this quiz as a tool to better understand how to care for yourself and others.

True *False*

☐ ☐ **1)** Antibiotics are the most effective treatment for the common cold, as well as the flu.

☐ ☐ **2)** An untreated case of strep throat could result in rheumatic fever.

☐ ☐ **3)** A fever of 104°F or higher that persists longer than 2 hours, needs medical attention.

☐ ☐ **4)** Hand washing is the most effective measure for preventing the spread of disease.

☐ ☐ **5)** A serious eye infection, or even blindness can result if a cold sore infects a person's eyes.

Answers can be found inside this section.

Introduction: Getting Started

Common Conditions

Common Conditions II

Relieving Aches & Pains

Chronic Conditions

Medical Consumerism

Getting Active

Managing Weight

Caring for
Common Conditions II

Ear Infections ★ Respiratory Conditions ★ Urinary Tract Infections ★ Vision Problems

Self-Care **ESSENTIALS**®
A SIMPLE GUIDE TO MANAGING YOUR HEALTH CARE AND LIVING WELL

Understanding **Ear Infections**

Introduction: Getting Started

Common Conditions

Common Conditions II

Relieving Aches & Pains

Chronic Conditions

Medical Consumerism

Getting Active

Managing Weight

About Ear Infections

Ear infections are caused by a buildup of fluid in the eustachian tube—a tube that drains fluid from the ears into the nasal passages. Ear infections are very common among young children, although they can occur in adults as well. It has been estimated that seven out of 10 children will have at least one ear infection by age three. A good portion of these children will have more than one ear infection. Ear infections occur in children most often, simply because childrens' eustachian tubes are shorter and less angled than are adult eustachian tubes, making blockage more likely when inflammation occurs.

Contrary to common fear, ear infections don't normally cause permanent hearing loss. However, if ear infections aren't treated conscientiously, it is possible for the infection to spread to the inner ear, where it can damage ear bones and the inner ear structure, causing permanent hearing damage.

With this in mind, it's important to treat your child's ear infection early and with a great deal of focus and determination. Doing so will better ensure a lifetime of proper hearing for you and/or your youngster.

Signs & Symptoms

Because ear infections often occur in young children, they may not always be able to communicate the situation clearly. Parents should be aware of nonverbal cues indicating that an infection is present. Increased irritability in your child, or pulling on the ear should clue parents in that an infection may be present.

Other symptoms include:

✓ Fever in an infant (younger than 3 months) greater than 100°F, or in an older child greater than 102°F

✓ Ear pain

✓ Increased crying in young children and infants

✓ Temporary hearing loss

✓ Sudden loss of appetite

✓ Preference for sleeping in an upright position

✓ Thick, yellow drainage from the ear, possibly including blood

A Self-Care Essential

Skip the Q-tip. Ear specialists recommend that cotton swabs NOT be used to clean ears, because they can be traumatic to the ear canal. Cotton swabs tend to force old skin, wax, and debris toward the eardrum, doing more harm than good. Try using a solution of white vinegar and rubbing alcohol applied with an ear dropper to remove wax. Don't use this method if you have a perforated eardrum.

When To Seek Care

If pain and discomfort lasts beyond two to three days, seek medical attention. Ear infections are commonly treated with antibiotics. Antibiotics usually clear up the infection within 10 days. After two to three days of taking the antibiotics, your child should begin to feel better. Even so, make sure that your child takes the antibiotics for the recommended amount of time to make sure the infection clears up properly.

Other signs that you should contact your healthcare provider include the following.

- If pain continues for more than two to three days after practicing self-care

- If your ear pain is severe, or getting worse

- See a doctor if your pain is accompanied by headaches, a stiff neck or back, fever, dementia, or irritability

- If the infection is present in an infant (younger than three months) with a fever of greater than 100°F or an older child with a fever of greater than 102°F

- If yellowish or bloody drainage is escaping from the ear

- If you notice redness or swelling behind the infected ear

Home Treatment

Most ear infections will run their course within a few days if self-care techniques are utilized. In fact, nearly 80 percent of ear infections clear up without any treatment at all. Use the following self-care techniques to address an ear infection properly.

- **Apply heat to the ear using a heating pad or warm washcloth.** Be sure the temperature is not too hot, and avoid this technique with very young children and infants.

- **Employ an over-the-counter medication** such as acetaminophen, or ibuprofen. Because of the risk of Reye's syndrome, **DO NOT GIVE ASPIRIN TO CHILDREN!**

- **Drink eight, 8 oz. glasses of clear fluids daily.**

- **Avoid getting water in the infected ear.**

- **Try using eardrops with a local anesthetic.** Eardrops should not be used if there is drainage from the ear.

Continued on the following page...

Introduction: Getting Started

Common Conditions

Common Conditions II

Relieving Aches & Pains

Chronic Conditions

Medical Consumerism

Getting Active

Managing Weight

Understanding **Ear Infections**

Continued...

Frequently Asked Questions

Take a look at the following frequently asked questions—they'll help you further understand this condition, and better care for yourself and your family.

Q **How common are ear infections?**
Ear infections in children are actually quite common. In fact, 70 percent of children will have at least one middle ear infection by the age of three. A good percentage of these children will have recurrent ear infections. Next to the common cold, ear infections just may be the most common illness in children.

Q **Why are children more prone to ear infections than adults?**
Because they have shorter, narrower eustachian tubes—the tubes that drain fluid from the inner ear. During an infection (like a common cold) the shorter, narrower eustachian tubes in children can become inflamed and swell more easily, trapping fluid and allowing bacteria to flourish.

Q **My child is experiencing recurrent ear infections. What are my options?**
Speak with your healthcare provider. Typically, antibiotics and time will heal ear infections, however, if ear infections become chronic, they can be dangerous and may lead to hearing loss and delayed speech development. In some cases, your doctor may recommend preventive antibiotic therapy or ear tubes to counteract this possibility.

Q **Do children outgrow ear infections?**
For the most part, yes. As a child grows and develops, eustachian tubes become wider and more angled, and therefore function better. Ear infections are still possible in older children and adults, but are much less common.

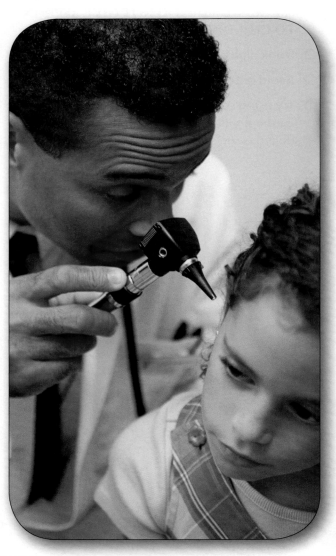

"Never stick anything deep into the ear canal as it can **damage the ear drum** and **may cause hearing loss**."

Side tabs: Introduction: Getting Started | Common Conditions | **Common Conditions II** | Relieving Aches & Pains | Chronic Conditions | Medical Consumerism | Getting Active | Managing Weight

Prevention

Ear infections, especially in younger children, are very hard, if not impossible to prevent. There are, however, a number of steps you can take to make them less likely. Practice the following tips to minimize your child's risk of an ear infection.

 Limit exposure to other children who have colds. Daycare centers can be breeding grounds for ear infections. Try a smaller daycare or keep your child at home if possible.

 Breast-feed your baby. Infants who are breast-fed have lower incidence of ear infections.

 Use care when bottle-feeding. Feeding infants while they're in an upright position can help to prevent ear infections.

 Wash hands frequently. Ear infections are usually the result of other infections like a cold or the flu. Keeping your hands clean can reduce your child's chances of coming down with an ear infection.

 Avoid cigarette smoke. Ear infections are more common in children who are exposed to cigarette smoke.

 Keep current on childhood immunizations. There is no specific immunization for ear infections, however, common immunizations may make your child more resistant to illnesses that may lead to later ear infections.

 Be careful when using a pacifier. Babies who continue to use their pacifiers after 12 months of age are more likely to develop ear infections.

Ear Tubes: Are they right for your child?

For children with severe and persistent ear infections, your healthcare provider may recommend ear tubes. Ear tubes are small, plastic tubes, strategically placed through the eardrum while a child is under general anesthetic. These tubes help ear infections by allowing air to enter the middle ear and by providing better drainage from the middle ear into the ear canal.

There are pros and cons to having ear tubes placed. Ultimately, the decision is up to you and your health care provider as to what will be best for your child.

Ear Tube Pros:
✓ Air can more easily enter the middle ear helping to clear the infection.

✓ Drainage is improved helping to clear and prevent infections.

✓ Pressure and pain of ear infections can be decreased.

✓ Hearing can be restored to some degree.

✓ Tubes can help to prevent future ear infections.

Ear Tube Cons:
✓ Child must be "put under" during the surgery.

✓ Tubes can be a hassle—while tubes are in place, water should not enter the ear (your child may have difficulty swimming, showering, etc.).

✓ The procedure might be frightening for your child.

✓ There is a small chance of scarring or a permanent perforation in the eardrum.

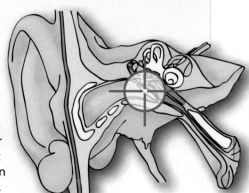

Introduction: Getting Started

Common Conditions

Common Conditions II

Relieving Aches & Pains

Chronic Conditions

Medical Consumerism

Getting Active

Managing Weight

Respiratory **Conditions**

About Respiratory Conditions

Allergies, bronchitis, and pneumonia are respiratory conditions that affect millions of Americans each year. In this section we'll learn about allergies, bronchitis, and pneumonia, learning when to employ self-care techniques, and when to contact a healthcare provider.

Allergies—an overreaction of the immune system to a normally harmless substance in the environment (called an allergen).

Bronchitis—an inflammation of the bronchial tubes leading to the lungs. Oftentimes, bronchitis appears within three to four days after an upper respiratory infection like a cold or the flu.

Pneumonia—an infection or inflammation that affects the bronchial tubes leading into the lungs. Pneumonia is typically the result of a bacterial infection, however, viruses and parasites can also cause this condition. Pneumonia sometimes follows a viral respiratory infection such as a cold or bronchitis.

Signs & Symptoms

Each of these conditions—allergies, bronchitis, and pneumonia—have similar symptoms, yet there are some important differences. Take a look at the symptoms for each condition outlined here to determine what you may be suffering from, and what you can do to find relief.

Allergies
✓ Itchy, watery eyes
✓ Nasal congestion
✓ Frequent sneezing
✓ A rash on the skin in the affected area

Bronchitis
✓ A dry cough that may later produce phlegm
✓ Mild fever
✓ Tiredness
✓ Tightness in the chest
✓ Difficulty breathing and/or wheezing

Pneumonia
✓ A cough producing yellow, green, or bloody sputum
✓ Moderate to intense fever accompanied by chills
✓ Rapid, shallow, or troubled breathing
✓ Rapid heart beat
✓ Pain in the chest when coughing
✓ Tiredness

"**Over 11 million Americans** are diagnosed with chronic bronchitis each year."

Introduction:
Getting Started

Common
Conditions

Common
Conditions II

Relieving
Aches & Pains

Chronic
Conditions

Medical
Consumerism

Getting
Active

Managing
Weight

✚ A Self-Care Essential

Get Treated Right Away. According to the American Lung Association, those with chronic bronchitis often neglect to get professional medical treatment when necessary because they don't think bronchitis can be serious. But in advanced stages, bronchitis can cause serious damage to the lungs and may lead to heart failure. If you experience any of the serious symptoms of bronchitis listed in this section, contact a healthcare provider right away.

When To Seek Care

Though most respiratory conditions are typically mild, they can become very serious, requiring the assistance of a healthcare professional. If you have any of the following symptoms, you should seek medical care immediately.

Allergies

⚕ If you have signs of anaphylactic shock, see a doctor immediately. Symptoms include hives all over the body, shortness of breath, tightness in the chest and/or throat, or swelling of the tongue or face.

⚕ If you become disoriented

⚕ If you become lightheaded or dizzy

⚕ If you develop diarrhea

⚕ If you are vomiting

Bronchitis

⚕ If chest pain is crushing or feels like a heavy weight on your chest (symptoms of a possible heart attack)

⚕ If your cough is accompanied by tightness in the chest or wheezing, or if your cough brings up green, yellow, or bloody sputum from the lungs for more than two days

⚕ If you are vomiting to the point of feeling faint

⚕ If you are having difficulty breathing or wheezing is increasing

⚕ If symptoms do not improve within 24-48 hours

Pneumonia

⚕ If you suspect you have pneumonia, contact your healthcare provider right away. Treatment for pneumonia almost always involves the use of antibiotics

⚕ If chest pain is crushing or feels like a heavy weight on your chest (symptoms of a possible heart attack)

⚕ If there is a bluish hue in your lips or fingertips

⚕ If your cough is accompanied by tightness in the chest or wheezing, or if your cough brings up green, yellow, or bloody sputum from the lungs for more than two days

⚕ If you are vomiting to the point of feeling faint

Continued on the following page...

Respiratory **Conditions**

Continued...

Home Treatment

Home treatment for most respiratory conditions is preferable as long as severe symptoms do not develop (see, "When to Seek Care" for a listing of severe symptoms). With proper care, it is possible to feel better within a week or two, except for cases of severe pneumonia, which may take several weeks to clear up.

Allergies

⌂ **Try over-the-counter antihistamines** like Claritin or Tavist.

⌂ **Use over-the-counter decongestants** like Sudafed or Neo-Synephrine.

⌂ **Try breathing steam** to clear nasal congestion.

⌂ **Use nonprescription nasal sprays, eye drops, and nose drops**—but not for more than three days.

Bronchitis

⌂ **Humidify your environment** to help ease congestion.

⌂ **Drink more fluids than usual**—at least eight, 8 oz. glasses of fluid per day.

⌂ **Try an over-the-counter cough medicine** for symptom relief.

⌂ **Use an over-the-counter pain reliever** such as ibuprofen or acetaminophen. Adults may take aspirin (never give aspirin to a child!).

Pneumonia

⌂ **If you suspect you have pneumonia, contact your healthcare provider right away.** Treatment for pneumonia almost always involves the use of antibiotics.

⌂ **Drink eight, 8 oz. glasses of fluid per day** to help bring mucus out of your lungs.

⌂ **Use an over-the-counter pain reliever** such as aspirin, ibuprofen, or acetaminophen to reduce fever and alleviate the accompanying body aches (never give aspirin to a child!).

⌂ **Try a nonprescription decongestant** to help soothe a cough.

⌂ **Try breathing steam** to clear nasal congestion.

Introduction: Getting Started

Common Conditions

Common Conditions II

Relieving Aches & Pains

Chronic Conditions

Medical Consumerism

Getting Active

Managing Weight

Frequently Asked Questions

Take a look at the following frequently asked questions—they'll help you further understand this condition, and better care for yourself and your family.

 I've heard that as I age, risk of serious complications from pneumonia increase. What can I do to reduce my risk?

You can get the pneumococcal vaccine. This vaccine is recommended for those age 65 or older, or those who have chronic health conditions such as asthma. The American Academy of Pediatrics recommends that children under two years of age also receive the pneumococcal vaccine.

 Does smoking cause bronchitis?

According to the American Lung Association smoking is by far the most common cause of chronic bronchitis. Smoking also causes heart disease, cancer, and emphysema. There's only one right thing to do when it comes to smoking—quit!

How can I tell the difference between a common cold and allergies?

Allergies and colds can often produce the same kinds of symptoms—runny nose, sneezing, congestion, etc. The main difference between the two is that an allergic reaction will most likely produce all symptoms at the same time. A cold, on the other hand, generally produces these symptoms in succession. Another way to distinguish allergies from a cold is to look at duration—colds typically last one week, whereas allergies will remain as long as the allergen is present.

Prevention

There are many things you can do reduce your chances of developing bronchitis or pneumonia, or to avoid allergic reactions. Take a look at some of the tips below.

Allergies

 Know your allergy triggers—like pet dander, pollen, or latex for example—and, if possible, avoid them.

 Keep your house and car windows closed.

 Don't smoke.

 Try using a HEPA filter on your air conditioner or air purifier (HEPA filters can reduce impurities in the air).

Bronchitis and Pneumonia

 Get a pneumococcal vaccination, especially if you are over the age of 65 or if you have a chronic condition such as asthma.

 Get a flu shot. Bronchitis and pneumonia can develop on the heels of a cold or the flu.

Stop smoking. Smoking is by far the most common cause of chronic bronchitis.

Get plenty of rest and increase your level of physical activity. Taking care of yourself can help to keep your immune system strong.

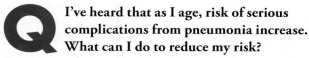

"Cigarette smoking is by far **the most common cause** of chronic bronchitis."

Introduction: Getting Started

Common Conditions

Common Conditions II

Relieving Aches & Pains

Chronic Conditions

Medical Consumerism

Getting Active

Managing Weight

Urinary **Tract Infections**

Introduction: Getting Started

Common Conditions

Common Conditions II

Relieving Aches & Pains

Chronic Conditions

Medical Consumerism

Managing Weight Active

About Urinary Tract Infections (UTIs)

Just as its name suggests, a urinary tract infection (UTI) is an infection of the urinary tract, which is comprised of the kidneys, the passageway between the kidneys and the bladder (ureter), the actual bladder, and a small tube that carries urine to the outside of your body (urethra). An infection of the urinary tract takes place most often when E. coli bacteria enter the urethra (the tube through which urine passes), and then enters your urine or bladder. The infection may then travel from the bladder to the ureter and finally to the kidneys.

Urinary tract infections are very common, and though not typically a serious medical condition, a UTI can be painful and uncomfortable. The following information can help you recognize, treat, and relieve the pain associated with a urinary tract infection.

An infection of the urinary tract takes place when bacteria from the digestive system adhere to the opening of the urethra and begin to multiply. The infection may then travel on to the bladder, the ureter, and finally to the kidneys. ▼

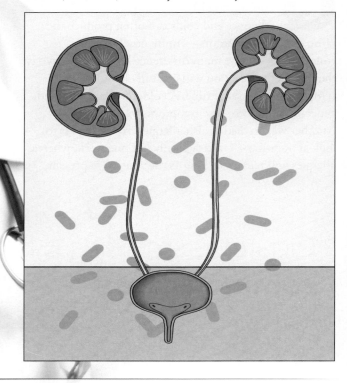

Introduction: Getting Started

Common Conditions

Common Conditions II

Relieving Aches & Pains

Chronic Conditions

Medical Consumerism

Getting Active

Managing Weight

✚ A Self-Care Essential

A Juicy Question. For years, cranberry juice has been consumed to treat and prevent urinary tract infections. And while the clinical evidence on the effectiveness of cranberry juice for treating UTIs remains mixed, the benefits of flushing your system with fluids to cleanse bacteria are well known. Make sure to drink plenty of fluids each day—cranberry juice or otherwise—when you have a UTI. The extra fluids will help cleanse your system.

Signs & Symptoms

The symptoms of UTIs are easy to identify. Consider the following signs and symptoms and determine whether or not you may be suffering from a UTI.

✓ Pain or burning during urination

✓ Frequent urges to urinate in small amounts

✓ Inability to control urine release

✓ Discolored urine (usually red or pink)

✓ Pain in the lower abdomen

✓ Urine that looks cloudy

✓ Unusual smelling urine

✓ Lower back pain on one side of the body

✓ Nausea, vomiting, fever, and/or chills

When To Seek Care

While most urinary tract infections can be treated easily at home, if symptoms persist or worsen, it's important that you see your healthcare provider. Untreated urinary tract infections can spread to other parts of the body such as the kidneys, and cause serious complications. If you're experiencing any of the following symptoms, see your healthcare provider right away.

⚕ If your symptoms last longer than one or two days following self-care treatment

⚕ If urination is extremely painful, and occurs with:

▸ A fever of 101°F or greater ▸ Nausea/vomiting

▸ Blood in the urine ▸ Fever and chills

▸ Discharge from the vagina or penis

⚕ See a healthcare provider if you experience lower back pain on one side of the body (commonly referred to as flank pain)

⚕ If you're pregnant

⚕ If you are unable to urinate despite a strong desire

⚕ If your young child is experiencing the symptoms of a UTI—especially if it is a second occurrence

Home Treatment

With quick attention and proper care, a urinary tract infection can be easily and effectively treated in the comfort of your own home. However, if your symptoms last longer than one or two days after beginning self-care, you should see your healthcare provider for treatment.

The following self-care techniques will help you treat a urinary tract infection at home.

⌂ **Drink plenty of fluids**—at least eight, 8 oz. glasses per day—especially in the first 24 hours. Forcing fluids can help to wash out bacteria causing the infection.

⌂ **Check your temperature twice daily**—a fever can indicate a serious infection that needs medical attention.

⌂ **Use a hot pad to soothe your genital area**—a warm bath may help, too (avoid harsh soaps and bubble baths).

⌂ **Urinate as often as possible and make sure to completely empty your bladder each time**—don't push too hard as it may cause injury.

⌂ **Avoid intimate activity and don't use a diaphragm**—until the infection clears.

Continued on the following page...

Urinary **Tract Infections**

Continued...

Frequently Asked Questions

Take a look at the following frequently asked questions—they'll help you further understand this condition, and better care for yourself and your family.

Q **What causes urinary tract infections?**
There are a lot of things that can cause a urinary tract infection. Bacteria from bowel movements can cause an infection if it makes its way into your urinary tract. For women, sexual intercourse can push bacteria into the bladder causing an infection. Those with diabetes may also be more susceptible to urinary tract infections because diabetes makes it harder for your body to fight off infection.

Q **If I have to go to the doctor for a UTI, what will he or she do?**
Because UTIs are so common, a trip to the doctor is really nothing to worry about. Your doctor will ask you to urinate into a cup, and the urine will be tested for the presence of an infection. If an infection is found, your doctor will most likely prescribe antibiotics to help clear up the infection.

Q **I've heard that pregnant women are more likely to suffer from a urinary tract infection. Is this true?**
Not necessarily. However, it may be more likely that the infection will travel to the kidneys in pregnant women. Doctors believe that the position of the urinary tract, along with hormonal changes that occur during pregnancy, make it easier for bacteria to travel through the ureters and into the kidneys.

Introduction: Getting Started

Common Conditions

Common Conditions II

Relieving Aches & Pains

Chronic Conditions

Medical Consumerism

Getting Active

Managing Weight

Prevention

While UTIs are extremely common, they aren't necessarily inevitable. There are some steps you can to take to avoid getting a urinary tract infection. And while the verdict is still out on the effectiveness of these prevention efforts, many who have suffered swear by the tips below.

Prevention For Adults

If you're a common sufferer give the following strategies a try:

 Drink eight, 8 oz. glasses of fluid per day.

 Urinate at the first feeling of need—do not wait until it's more convenient to urinate.

 Wear cotton underwear to keep dry, and loose clothing to allow skin to breathe.

 If you use a diaphragm, keep it clean and checked regularly for proper fitting.

 Avoid intercourse until the infection clears.

Prevention In Children

Your child's well-being is always a concern, so it's important to treat a UTI in children as early as possible, and also take steps to prevent them from occurring.

The following steps can help prevent UTIs in children.

 Don't give your child bubble baths—soapy solutions are perfect places for bacteria to thrive.

 Be sure your child wears loose fitting clothing—this includes underwear.

 If you have a girl, make sure she wipes from front to back when using the bathroom.

 If you have an uncircumcised boy, make sure he knows how to wash his foreskin properly.

 Be sure that your child makes adequate trips to the bathroom.

"Drinking at least **eight, 8 oz. glasses of fluids** daily can help flush the bacteria causing a UTI."

Treating **Vision Problems**

About Vision Problems

Although vision problems can be uncomfortable and sometimes frightening, most are not serious. In fact, the three common vision problems discussed here—dry eyes, pink eye (conjunctivitis), and styes—are quite common and are usually not cause for alarm.

Signs & Symptoms

Dry Eyes

In addition to the natural drying of our eyes with age, allergies, smoke, dust, and some medications (sleeping aids, blood pressure pills, etc.) can cause dry eyes. Symptoms include:

✓ Eyes that feel hot and gritty when blinking

✓ Eyes that are irritated and slightly red

✓ Difficulty closing the eyelid

Pink Eye (Conjunctivitis)

Pink eye is an inflammation of the membrane (conjunctiva) that lines the eyelid and eyeball. Bacteria, viruses, and irritants in the air can cause pink eye. Symptoms include:

✓ One or both eyes become red and/or itchy

✓ Sensitivity to light

✓ Slightly blurred vision

✓ Eye discharge that may "crust over" as you sleep

Styes

A sty is a non-contagious infection of an eyelash follicle. Normally, styes fill with pus for about a week and then burst. Symptoms include:

✓ Itchy eyelid

✓ Red bump on the eye lid

"See a doctor immediately if you experience **sudden, partial, or total loss of vision**."

Introduction: Getting Started

Common Conditions

Common Conditions II

Relieving Aches & Pains

Chronic Conditions

Medical Consumerism

Getting Active

Managing Weight

Introduction: Getting Started

Common Conditions

Common Conditions II

Relieving Aches & Pains

Chronic Conditions

Medical Consumerism

Getting Active

Managing Weight

✚ A Self-Care Essential

Picking the Right Pair of Sunglasses. Are darker lenses in sunglasses more protective than lighter lenses? No. Tint has nothing to do with it. What you want to look for is adequate protection against both UVA and UVB light. Look for a sticker on your sunglasses that reads, "Z80.3." These sunglasses meet various protection standards set by the American National Standards Institute.

When To Seek Care

There are some general eye symptoms that require immediate, emergency attention. Seek medical attention in the following situations.

General

⚕ If you experience sudden, partial, or total loss of vision. Seek medical attention immediately in this case—minutes can mean the difference between healthy eyes and vision loss.

⚕ If you experience severely blurred vision and colored halos around bright objects (sign of sudden glaucoma).

⚕ If you notice a veil-like filter covering your field of vision or you see flashes of light appear in one eye (sign of retinal detachment).

Dry Eyes

⚕ If your condition persists despite self-care treatments.

Pink Eye

⚕ See a doctor if there is pain in the eye(s), blurred vision, or a loss of vision.

⚕ If you feel like there's something in your eye.

⚕ If yellow, green, or bloody discharge accompanies redness of the eye(s).

⚕ If pupils are different sizes.

⚕ If pink eye does not respond to self-care or if symptoms last longer than one week.

Sty

⚕ If sty pain is severe or if a sty quickly increases in size.

⚕ If the sty does not respond to self-care treatment within one week.

⚕ If the sty seems to be affecting the entire eye or eyeball.

Home Treatment

Dry Eyes

Try the following strategies to gain relief from dry eyes.

⌂ **Blink your eyes as often as you can.**

⌂ **Avoid eye irritants such as smoke or dust.**

⌂ **Use over-the-counter eye drops** like Allergan or Aqua Site to help relieve dry eyes.

Pink Eye

If you experience any symptoms of pink eye, contact your healthcare provider. Your healthcare provider may test the secretions from your eye to determine whether the cause is viral or bacterial. Viral pink eye will usually clear up on its own, while bacterial pink eye will require an antibiotic eyedrop or ointment.

Sty

Use the following self-care tips to treat a sty.

⌂ **Apply a warm compress to the sty** four to five times daily for 10 minutes to ease pain.

⌂ **Do not squeeze a sty,** or attempt to pop it. If it does burst, let it do so on its own.

⌂ **If the sty bursts, rinse your eye thoroughly.**

DO YOU KNOW HOW TO CARE FOR...

Common Conditions?

Take The Self-Care Quiz

The quiz below is designed to test your knowledge on the information presented in this section. Use this quiz as a tool to better understand how to care for yourself and others.

True *False*

☐ ☐ **1)** Ear infections are most common among children.

☐ ☐ **2)** Dark lenses in sunglasses are more protective.

☐ ☐ **3)** Cigarette smoking is by far the most common cause of chronic bronchitis.

☐ ☐ **4)** Urinary tract infections are very rare.

☐ ☐ **5)** You should "pop" a sty as soon as you find it.

Answers can be found inside this section.

Introduction: Getting Started

Common Conditions

Common Conditions II

Relieving Aches & Pains

Chronic Conditions

Medical Consumerism

Getting Active

Managing Weight

Relieving
Aches and Pains

Back Pain ★ Headaches ★ Abdominal Pain ★ Managing Pain

Self-Care **ESSENTIALS**®
A SIMPLE GUIDE TO MANAGING YOUR HEALTH CARE AND LIVING WELL

Understanding **Back Pain**

Introduction:
Getting Started

Common
Conditions

Common
Conditions II

**Relieving
Aches & Pains**

Chronic
Conditions

Medical
Consumerism

Getting
Active

Managing
Weight

About Back Pain

Eighty percent of us will experience back problems at some point in our lives. Back pain is ranked second only to headaches as the most frequent cause of pain, and tops the list of workplace injuries, causing more lost time, disability, and lost dollars than any other workplace injury.

Our backs are a carefully engineered network of bones, tendons, ligaments, and nerves that help balance and bear the weight of our bodies and the loads we carry. Any minor damage or imbalance to this delicate system can stress muscles and joints, causing pain and injury. A lifetime of poor posture, poor lifting, bending and reaching, and twisting activities can gradually weaken your back's supportive structures as well as cause pain and injury.

Risk Factors For Back Pain

Being overweight. Your back has to support too much weight when you're carrying extra pounds.

Poor muscle tone. If your muscles are not well toned, they can't meet the challenge when you ask something extra of them.

Poor posture. Poor posture creates bodily stress, which can result in pain.

Improper lifting. Heavy lifting, carrying children, as well as occupational lifting can cause injury.

Desk jobs/computer use. Our bodies don't thrive sitting for long periods of time hunched over keyboards or other workspaces.

Unhappiness. Researchers have found that general dissatisfaction with our social and economic situations can double or triple the risk of low back pain.

With all these risk factors, it's no wonder so many of us suffer from back pain. But it's not a part of life you have to passively accept.

Read on to learn a little more about back pain including symptoms, home treatment, when to see a doctor, as well as how to prevent back pain in the first place.

Back pain is ranked second only to headaches as the most frequent cause of pain, and tops the list of workplace injuries.

A Self-Care Essential

Crunch Time. To ease pain in the back, try strengthening your stomach muscles by doing "crunch" type sit-ups. Here's how to do them properly.

▶ **Lie flat on your back.** Sit up far enough to lift only your upper back off the floor—not your whole upper body.

▶ **Go slowly.** Moving slowly forces your stomach muscles to work harder.

Doing crunches properly (going slowly and not sitting up all the way) can strengthen your stomach muscles, and may provide relief from back pain. Check with your healthcare professional before taking on an exercise program.

Signs & Symptoms

Most back pain is the result of strained or overworked muscles and ligaments (other causes may include arthritis, osteoporosis, and urinary tract infections). The most common symptoms of simple back sprains and strains are listed below. They include:

✓ Muscle spasms   ✓ Stiffness

✓ Cramping

✓ Pain that develops quickly or over a long period of time

✓ Pain that's aggravated by specific or repeated movements

When To Seek Care

There are some tell tale signs indicating that you're experiencing something more serious than a simple backache. See a healthcare provider if you experience any of the following conditions.

☤ If the back pain is extremely severe, spans the width of your upper back, and came on quickly with no apparent cause (these conditions can be a sign of more serious issues than just back pain)

☤ If the pain started near your chest and moved to your upper back (this may be an indication that you are experiencing a heart attack)

☤ If the pain in your back is severe and was brought on by a specific injury or fall

☤ If your back pain is accompanied by weakness or numbness in your legs

☤ If back pain is followed by bladder or bowel control problems

☤ If your pain or stiffness persists past 2 weeks of home treatment or if you are unable to stand erect

☤ If the pain is in a bone or joint and persists for more than three days

Home Treatment

Because most back pain is the result of minor muscle and ligament sprains and strains, the majority of back pain can be treated simply and inexpensively in your own home. If you're experiencing minor back pain, try some of the following strategies for relief.

⌂ **Rest!** At the first sign of back pain, stop what you're doing to prevent aggravating the situation, and stretch lightly. For acute pain, rest on a firm mattress for 48 hours. Thereafter, avoid activities that hurt, but don't stop moving entirely. Inactivity may cause your muscles to weaken and could prolong the healing process.

⌂ **Apply ice.** After an injury, immediately apply ice (wrapped in a towel) several times a day for up to 20 minutes at a time. Once acute pain has subsided, usually within the first two days, apply heat using a heating pad or hot water bag for approximately 20 minutes per session.

⌂ **Massage.** Massage can increase circulation and flexibility, reduce tension and pain, and help relieve muscle spasms.

⌂ **Use stress reduction techniques.** Many healthcare providers believe back pain has a lot more to do with stress than structural problems. Use relaxation tapes, humorous movies, meditation, and other stress reduction methods while you recuperate.

⌂ **Medicate.** Take an over-the-counter, nonsteroidal, anti-inflammatory medication such as aspirin or ibuprofen (Advil), which reduces inflammation in the joints and muscles, as well as helps to relieve pain. Acetaminophen (Tylenol) is another great pain reliever. Do not give aspirin to children.

Continued on the following page...

Introduction: Getting Started

Common Conditions

Common Conditions II

Relieving Aches & Pains

Chronic Conditions

Medical Consumerism

Getting Active

Managing Weight

Understanding **Back Pain**

Continued...

Frequently Asked Questions

Take a look at the following frequently asked questions—they'll help you further understand this condition, and better care for yourself and your family.

Q **Do I need surgery for my bad back?**
No, not usually. More times than not, your back pain can be treated without going under the knife. However, some conditions, like a herniated disk, may benefit from surgery. Even still,

herniated disks may heal on their own. Bottom line—you should carefully consider your options, and then consider them again, before thinking about surgery.

Q **What about alternative therapy?**
Nontraditional therapy is becoming more widely accepted these days. It wasn't long ago that chiropractic treatment was viewed as an "alternative" therapy. Now these specialists are a common part of the back care landscape. Other alternative therapies have received praise from sufferers, too. The choice is up to you.

Q **I sit at a desk all day. Am I at risk for back pain and injury?**
Yes. It's a common misconception that physical laborers and construction workers are at a higher risk for back injuries. The fact is, those individuals in sedentary jobs are at risk for back injury, too. Exercise and regular movement are important factors in maintaining a healthy back.

Q **How can I arrange my office environment to protect my back?**
A chair with good back support and height adjusters that allow you to keep both feet flat on the floor can do wonders to keep your back in a healthy state. If you don't have an adjustable chair, try to use a chair with a simple straight back whenever possible. Also, when it comes to your desk, arrange items (phone, keyboard, monitor, etc.) where you won't have to twist and turn excessively to access them.

Q **Will my back pain ever go away?**
There's good news and bad news. First the good news. With proper self-care and good prevention techniques you can be well on your way to fighting off back pain. Now the bad news. Considering that 80 percent of Americans experience back pain at some point in their lives—much of it recurring—you may never get rid of back pain altogether. That's why it's important to practice the prevention tips included in this section—and keep doing them even when you're feeling better.

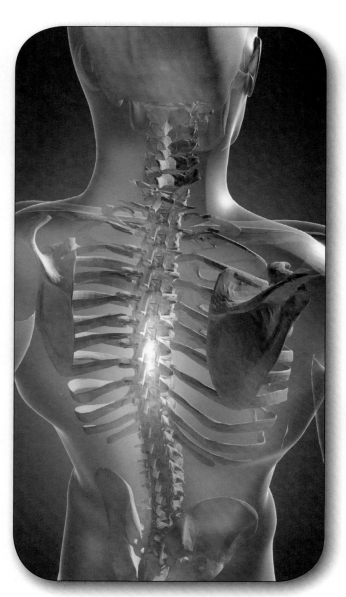

Introduction: Getting Started

Common Conditions

Common Conditions II

Relieving Aches & Pains

Chronic Conditions

Medical Consumerism

Getting Active

Managing Weight

"With **60% of the population** now obese or overweight, reports of back pain will almost certainly be on the rise."

Prevention

Once you've experienced an acute episode of back pain, you're five times more likely to suffer another episode. You can reduce this risk and the risk of back pain in general by making some of the important lifestyle changes outlined below—be sure to work with your healthcare provider in advance to ensure your health and safety.

 Exercise and control weight. Exercise is one of the best weapons against back problems. Aerobic exercise such as walking, swimming, jogging, or bicycling will help you control your weight, enhance your overall fitness, reduce stress, and improve your aerobic capacity. Eating right helps control excess weight, which increases stress on your back causing or aggravating back pain.

 Stretch. Proper stretching reduces the risk of injury by warming up tight muscles, increasing circulation, and maintaining flexibility. It's important whether you're going out for a jog, or just getting ready to do chores around the house.

 Strengthen your back. Doing exercises to strengthen your lower back as well as other supporting muscles will help reduce wear and tear on your back, and make you less prone to other injuries. Before starting a new exercise program, consult a healthcare professional who can help you develop a personalized plan of your own.

 Maintain good posture. Poor posture while sitting and standing (slouching or standing with a swayback) exaggerates your back's natural curves and puts unnecessary strain on your back. Stand and sit up straight by pulling in your stomach muscles, pushing shoulders back, and keeping your feet flat on the ground when sitting.

The 10-Minute Home Stretch

Keeping a healthy back means incorporating stretching into your daily routine. Here are a few key exercises to concentrate on. Remember, never stretch cold muscles. Make sure to get some blood flowing first by walking or doing some quick deep knee bends or jumping jacks for approximately 60 to 90 seconds.

Exercise #1:
Knee To Shoulder

Lie on your back with your knees bent, feet flat on the floor, and arms at your sides. Grasp your right knee and gently pull it up toward your right shoulder. Return to the starting position and repeat the exercise with your left leg.

Exercise #2:
Seated Trunk Flexion

Sitting near the edge of a chair, spread your legs and cross your arms over your chest. Tuck your chin and slowly curl your trunk downward. Relax. Uncurl slowly into an upright position, raising your head last.

Exercise #3:
Press Up

Lie on your stomach with your hands in position as if preparing for a push-up. Slowly lift your torso while keeping your hips and legs down and in contact with the floor. Raise your torso, slowly increasing the lower back curve to a point where you feel a stretch, then lower yourself back down to the starting position. Repeat.

Introduction: Getting Started

Common Conditions

Common Conditions II

Relieving Aches & Pains

Chronic Conditions

Medical Consumerism

Getting Active

Managing Weight

Relieving **Headaches**

About Headaches

If you suffer from regular headaches, you're not alone. Nearly 90 percent of the population has had at least one headache in the last year, and many sufferers experience not only the pain, but also the diminished quality of life, and out-of-pocket expenses, which add up fast. In fact, it is estimated that Americans spend more than $4 billion each year on over-the-counter pain relievers to ease their headaches.

The good news—in the last 20 years, medical research has identified new insights into pain management. The new understanding has led to advances in treatment and renewed hope for longtime sufferers.

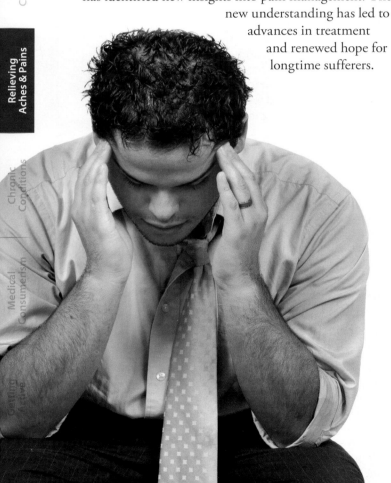

Types of Headaches

Although there are different types of headaches—150 to be exact—tension headaches and migraine headaches are the most common.

Tension headaches. Tension headaches are experienced by as many as 90 percent of adults, and are the most common kind of headache. Also known as muscle contraction or stress headaches, tension headaches are typically associated with a dull, aching pain that affects both sides of the head.

Migraine headaches. The second most common type of headache, migraines affect approximately 28 million Americans. Migraine headaches typically affect one side of the head, have a pulsating or throbbing sensation, and are often accompanied by nausea or vomiting and sensitivity to light and sound.

Signs & Symptoms

Tension or Migraine?

Now that we know a little more about the two main types of headaches, let's learn about each in detail, getting a better grasp on the symptoms associated with each. The following symptoms will help you better distinguish between tension headaches and migraine headaches.

Tension Headache

✓ Mild to moderate pain or throbbing in the forehead, above the ears, or near the back of the head

✓ Accompanied by neck and shoulder pain

✓ Begins gradually, usually near mid-day

✓ May last anywhere from 30 minutes to several days

✓ Accompanied by irritability, trouble concentrating, and sensitivity to noise and/or light

Migraine Headache

✓ Moderate to severe pain, often affecting only one side of the head

✓ Nausea, vomiting, and upset stomach

✓ Extreme sensitivity to light and/or sound

✓ Blurred vision   ✓ Dizziness

✓ Fatigue   ✓ Loss of appetite

Introduction: Getting Started

Common Conditions

Common Conditions II

Relieving Aches & Pains

Chronic Conditions

Medical Consumerism

Getting Active

Introduction: Getting Started

Common Conditions

Common Conditions II

Relieving Aches & Pains

Chronic Conditions

Medical Consumerism

Getting Active

Managing Weight

✚ A Self-Care Essential

Three Tips for Fighting Migraines. The severity of migraine pain has led people to explore a variety of treatment options. Here are three treatment options you may want to consider if you're dealing with migraine pain.

▸ **Icing:** Reusable ice packs wrapped around the head may help soothe pain.

▸ **Massage:** Have someone gently rub the muscles in your neck, back, and temples.

▸ **Relax:** If you can master one of the many relaxation techniques (meditation, guided imagery, etc.), it may reduce stress and relieve pain to some degree.

Remember, when it comes to migraines, do what works best for you. Consult with your healthcare provider and experiment cautiously to reduce pain.

When To Seek Care

There are times when your headache becomes more than just an annoyance. Severe headaches that are long-lasting and accompanied by some of the symptoms listed here can be a sign of a more serious condition. See your healthcare provider right away if your headache includes any the following characteristics.

☤ If the headache is accompanied by fever, stiff neck, confusion, seizures, double vision, weakness, numbness, or difficulty speaking and/or understanding

☤ If the headache is severe and cannot be relieved with home treatment

☤ If your unexplained headaches continue to occur more than three times a week

☤ If your headaches strike suddenly or severely

☤ If headaches occur during or after physical exertion, sexual activity, coughing, or sneezing

☤ If your headaches awaken you from a sound sleep or are worse first thing in the morning

Home Treatment

There are a number of ways you can help to ensure headaches don't take you out of the game. The following suggestions can help you take control of a headache before it takes control of you.

⌂ **Try taking an over-the-counter pain reliever** such as acetaminophen (Tylenol), aspirin (Bayer), ibuprofen (Motrin), or naproxen (Aleve) as soon as you feel that a headache is coming on. Be sure to follow label directions to prevent rebound headaches. Do not give aspirin to children.

⌂ **When you feel a headache coming on, retreat to a dark, quiet place and relax.** Often times, a small nap can relieve your headache.

⌂ **Massage your own shoulders or neck**, or have someone give you a hand.

⌂ **Place a cool, wet towel or cold pack on the location of your headache or forehead.**

⌂ **Do not apply heat**—it tends to intensify headaches.

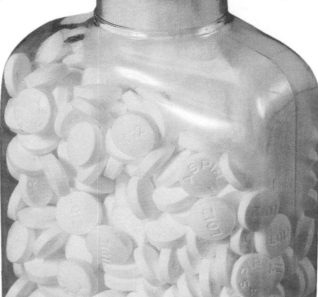

Continued on the following page…

Relieving **Headaches**

Continued...

Frequently Asked Questions

Take a look at the following frequently asked questions—they'll help you further understand this condition, and better care for yourself and your family.

Q **Can headaches be prevented?**
Although not every headache can be prevented altogether, paying attention to things like reducing stress, exercising regularly, quitting smoking, and avoiding headache "triggers," can help you reduce the frequency and severity of your headaches.

Q **I've heard that relaxation exercises can help treat headaches. What types of relaxation methods are recommended?**
Using relaxation techniques like rhythmic breathing, deep breathing, visualized breathing, progressive muscle relaxation, listening to music, and guided imagery can be a big help for those suffering from tension headaches. Keep in mind, however, that there is no perfect recipe for relaxation; you'll have to do what works best for you.

Q **What are rebound headaches, and which medications are most responsible for causing them?**
Rebound headaches are constant, low-grade headaches that often will not go away. It is thought that the use of common over-the-counter medications—when taken in large quantities and over a long period of time—can cause rebound headaches. Aspirin, acetaminophen, Anacin, and Excedrin, can be very effective when taken as directed, but be careful not to overdo it. Do not give aspirin to children.

Q **I've heard that certain foods and beverages can trigger headaches. Which ones should I look out for?**
Alcohol—especially beer, whiskey, champagne, and red wine—can cause headaches because of the impurities it contains, and because alcohol increases blood flow to the brain. Cold foods like ice cream or cold beverages may also trigger headaches. You may also want to watch out for food additives like nitrates, which can dilate blood vessels and bring about headaches in some people.

Q **Are migraines hereditary?**
Yes. Unfortunately, migraine headaches run in families. It's been estimated that if one parent has a history of migraines, the child has a 50/50 chance of having migraines as well.

If both parents suffer from migraines, then there's a 75 percent chance that the child will have migraines, too.

Q **What about caffeine, is it good or bad for my headache?**
It appears to be both. According to some researchers, caffeine is good for your headache. A widely accepted substance for treating headaches, caffeine has been found in many prescription and over-the-counter headache medicines. According to some research, caffeine makes pain relievers 40 percent more effective in treating headaches. Too much caffeine, however, (for example taking medication and drinking excessive amounts of coffee) may increase your chances for rebound headaches.

Prevention

Most would agree, an occasional headache is probably just a fact of life. That being said, nobody should have to deal with frequent and severe headaches. The following prevention techniques should be employed if you'd like to cope more effectively with headaches.

 Reduce emotional stress. Take time to relax before and after stressful situations (headache triggers) that have caused headaches in the past.

 Reduce physical stress. Be sure to get plenty of rest each night so you are better prepared to face stress each day. If you sit at a desk, stretch often. Become aware of jaw clenching and tightness in the neck and shoulders and work to eliminate these habits.

 Exercise on a regular basis. Try to get at least 30 minutes of moderate exercise on most days of the week.

 Keep a headache diary. Even though it may be a hassle to write down when your headaches occur, suspected triggers, the severity and location of the pain, and any other related symptoms, doing so can help you learn more about your headaches, and hopefully, prevent them in the future.

Treating **Abdominal Pain**

About Abdominal Pain

Most abdominal pain is not serious, although it can be extremely uncomfortable. Diarrhea, constipation, and excessive gas are common causes of abdominal pain. Fortunately, these conditions can be treated at home using simple self-care techniques. Treatment depends on which of these conditions you are experiencing.

Signs & Symptoms

Oftentimes, the symptoms of diarrhea, constipation, and gas can be similar, and may even be experienced together. Take a closer look at the symptoms outlined here to determine which condition you may be experiencing.

Diarrhea

✓ More than three or four loose, watery stools per day

✓ Cramping or pain in the abdomen

✓ Bloating

Constipation

✓ Difficulty passing stools

✓ Firm, hard bowel movements

✓ Cramping and pain in the rectum

Gas

✓ Rumbling in the stomach

✓ Excessive flatulence (more than 20 per day)

✓ Inability to pass gas

✓ Bloating

"There's no single way to prevent gas altogether, but **paying close attention to what you eat**, and how your body reacts to it, is a good first step."

A Self-Care Essential

Remember the Two-Hour Rule. Abdominal pain is often linked to food poisoning—remember the two-hour rule. Leaving food at room temperature for more than two hours is dangerous—bacteria grow rapidly between 40°F and 140°F. Remember to refrigerate leftovers immediately after eating. Use shallow containers to speed cooling. Also, the USDA recommends that food left in the fridge for more than three to five days be discarded.

When To Seek Care

Most abdominal pain is more of an annoyance than a serious medical condition. However, there are times when your condition may indicate the presence of a more serious health problem. Seek medical attention if you're experiencing any of the following symptoms.

Diarrhea
- If you have diarrhea that lasts longer than 1 week
- If you become dehydrated—symptoms include little or no urination, weakness or dizziness, and an excessively dry mouth
- If stools are bloody
- If you have a fever of 101.5°F or higher with diarrhea

Constipation
- If stools are thin and pencil-like (can indicate the presence of a tumor in the lower bowel)
- If your constipation lasts longer than three weeks
- If stools are bloody
- If you are reliant on laxatives for bowel movements

Gas
- If your gas is accompanied by crushing or squeezing chest pain (possible sign of a heart attack)
- If gas is associated with pain that spreads to the upper abdomen, back, jaw, or arms (possible sign of a heart attack)
- If your gas is accompanied by severe, steady pain in the upper abdomen

Home Treatment

Home treatment for most abdominal pain is relatively straightforward, and most often involves taking an over-the-counter medication to relieve symptoms.

Diarrhea
- **Drink eight, 8 oz. glasses of water or other clear fluids** such as clear soda, juices, or tea each day.
- **As your diarrhea clears, add semisolid and low-fiber foods to your diet.**
- **Avoid dairy products, fatty, or seasoned foods.**
- **Stay away from caffeine and nicotine.**
- **Try an over-the-counter medication** such as Pepto-Bismol or Imodium.

Constipation
- **Eat on a regular schedule if possible,** and consume more high-fiber foods such as fruits and vegetables.
- **Drink eight, 8 oz. glasses of water or other clear fluids** such as clear soda, juices, or tea each day.
- **Increase your level of physical activity.**
- **If necessary, try a laxative such as Metamucil or Milk of Magnesia.** (Be sure to follow label directions as excessive use of laxatives can actually be harmful and make your constipation worse).

Gas
- **Avoid eating spicy or fatty foods.**
- **Eat slowly, and avoid excessive air intake.**
- **Cut down on carbonated drinks and beer.**
- **Avoid lying down immediately after eating.**
- **Increase your level of physical activity.**
- **Try an over-the-counter medication** such as Gas-X to relieve symptoms.

Continued on the following page...

Treating **Abdominal Pain**

Continued...

Frequently Asked Questions

Take a look at the following frequently asked questions—they'll help you further understand this condition, and better care for yourself and your family.

Q **I hear that a normal person has a bowel movement at least once a day. Is this true?**
No. In fact, anywhere from three times a day to three times a week is considered "normal."

What you should be most concerned with is what is most normal for you. Your bowel frequency may change slightly from time to time, which is nothing to worry about. Drastic changes, however, may be cause to seek medical advice.

Q **What's the best way to prevent gas?**
There's no single way to prevent gas altogether, but paying close attention to what you eat, and how your body reacts to it, is a good first step. Watch also what you drink. Carbonated drinks such as soda and beer can cause gas. Be sure to get plenty of exercise, as this will help your body eliminate gas in a healthy, natural way.

Q **I tend to get traveler's diarrhea every year. How can I avoid it?**
Traveler's diarrhea is common among international travelers (in fact 20 to 50 percent of these travelers will experience traveler's diarrhea). But traveler's diarrhea is not just limited to international travelers; anyone is at risk if eating undercooked food from street vendors and even food at buffets. In all of these conditions, bacteria are present and can cause traveler's diarrhea. Simply stated, watch what you eat when you travel to avoid traveler's diarrhea.

*"Traveler's diarrhea is not just limited to international travelers; anyone is at risk if eating **undercooked food from street vendors** and even **food at buffets**."*

Introduction: Getting Started

Common Conditions

Common Conditions II

Relieving Aches & Pains

Chronic Conditions

Medical Consumerism

Getting Active

Managing Weight

Introduction: Getting Started

Common Conditions

Common Conditions II

Relieving Aches & Pains

Chronic Conditions

Medical Consumerism

Getting Active

Managing Weight

Prevention

Many abdominal pains, especially those caused by diarrhea, constipation, and gas, can easily be prevented by following a few simple lifestyle guidelines. To reduce your incidence of abdominal pain, try the following:

 Eat a well-balanced diet that includes plenty of fruits and vegetables, as well as many high-fiber foods.

 Be sure to get plenty of fluids, including eight, 8oz. glasses of water each day to remain fully hydrated.

 Cut down on carbonated beverages such as soda or beer.

 Avoid chewing gum (sometimes causes you to swallow air).

 Avoid eating spicy, seasoned, or high-fat foods.

 Increase your level of physical activity—30 minutes of moderate exercise most days of the week is the recommended amount.

What Causes Ulcers?

For years, stomach ulcers were a mystery—nobody really knew what caused them. Some thought it had much to do with diet, while others believed excessive smoking and drinking was the culprit. And almost everyone suspected stress.

As it turns out, everybody was right—almost. While lifestyle factors, such as those mentioned above, make ulcers more likely to appear, ulcers are actually caused by a bacteria named H. pylori. Some ulcers are also caused by overuse of aspirin and other over-the-counter pain relievers.

An ulcer is a sore in the lining of the digestive track that can be quite painful. Burning pain in the abdomen is frequent with an ulcer, as are dark, red stools caused by bleeding in the stomach. If you suspect that you have an ulcer, make an appointment to see your healthcare provider. He or she can provide a treatment regimen that's right for you.

Of course, prevention is always the best route to take. Make ulcers less likely by quitting smoking, limiting alcohol use, and watching the amount of over-the-counter pain relievers you consume.

Is Your Stomach Pain Appendicitis?

Appendicitis is an inflammation of the appendix, a small, hollow sac attached to the large intestine. The appendix is located in the lower right area of the abdomen. Fortunately, a very specific sequence of events will usually occur if you have appendicitis.

If appendicitis is the cause of your pain, the first symptom you will most likely experience is pain near the belly button or just below the breastbone. Next, you may experience nausea and vomiting. You may also lose your appetite. The third symptom you will most likely experience with appendicitis is pain in the lower, right corner of your abdomen. Finally, you will experience a fever between 100°F and 102°F.

Remember, these are the classic signs and symptoms of appendicitis—if you suspect you have appendicitis, contact your healthcare provider right away.

Managing **Pain**

About Managing Pain

Pain is a well-known fact of life, and for many of us, an all-too-common occurrence in daily living. Pain is actually a warning signal—our body's way of telling us something isn't quite right. Without pain, we would have no way of knowing about serious, medical conditions ongoing in our bodies, and treatment of these conditions could be significantly delayed.

General pain comes in two varieties—acute and chronic.

Acute pain can usually be diagnosed and treated, and is usually confined to a given period of time and level of severity. Examples of acute pain include cutting your finger, or bumping your head.

Chronic pain persists over a long period of time and is resistant to most medical treatments. Chronic pain severely limits life enjoyment. Examples of chronic pain include arthritis, backaches, and sometimes conditions that are difficult to identify.

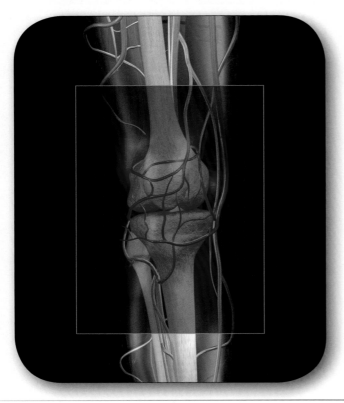

Managing Your Pain

There are literally hundreds of techniques used to manage pain. Three of the most common and universally accepted methods are discussed here. Keep in mind, when it comes to managing your pain, work with your healthcare provider to determine which strategy works best for you.

Pain Relievers/Medications (analgesics)—
Common pain relievers include substances like ibuprofen, acetaminophen, and aspirin. These substances can be effective in treating both acute and chronic pain if used according to label directions. Common pain relievers work by blocking the production of prostaglandin (prass-tih-glan-din)—a chemical that tells the brain the location and severity of the pain.

Physical Therapy—
If you have chronic pain, or are recovering from an accident or medical procedure that causes bouts of acute pain, you may benefit from seeing a physical therapist. A physical therapist is a highly-trained professional who works with individuals to reduce pain through range of motion exercises, stretching, strength training, and general exercise. If you think your pain may be reduced by working with a physical therapist, ask your healthcare provider about a referral.

Exercise—
A specifically prescribed exercise regimen is increasingly becoming a part of most healthcare providers' recommendations for the treatment of pain. Because many types of chronic pain are linked with tense, weak muscles, exercise—even light exercise—has proven itself effective in contributing to an overall sense of well-being by improving blood and oxygen flow to the muscles. It's important, however, that you follow your healthcare provider's specific recommendations to avoid further injury and greater pain.

> "When treating aches and pains **get plenty of rest**, but stay cautiously active— **prolonged rest may cause muscles to weaken**."

Introduction: Getting Started

Common Conditions

Common Conditions II

Relieving Aches & Pains

Chronic Conditions

Medical Consumerism

Getting Active

Managing Weight

A Self-Care Essential

Running Hot and Cold. Finding relief from chronic or acute pain may sometimes be as simple as applying heat or cold to the affected area. Try using an ice pack to reduce pain related to inflammation. Using a heating pad or a water bottle to apply heat to an affected area should help relieve muscle tension and cramps. Apply heat or cold as needed for 20 minutes at a time. You may find that either heat or cold works better for your pain management. If so, stick with it.

When To Seek Care

Acute Pain

Because acute pain is often associated with specific medical conditions, when to see a healthcare provider depends on the type of condition you're experiencing. Do some research and speak with a healthcare professional to learn more. Keep in mind that sudden, severe pain—the worst pain you've ever experienced—is always a medical emergency, and reason to call 911.

Chronic Pain

If you're experiencing chronic pain, contact your healthcare provider in the following situations.

- If your pain has lasted for more than three months

- If you are feeling depressed and having a hard time enjoying life experiences

- If chronic pain is keeping you up at night

- If you have recovered from an illness, yet pain associated with the illness lingers

Three Tips For Finding Relief

1 Learn About Your Condition—

There's no substitute for being well-educated about the causes of your pain and how to manage it. Several resources exist—friends and family, online resources, and your healthcare provider—that can help you learn all you need to know about your condition.

2 Communicate Clearly With Your Healthcare Provider—

Finding a healthcare provider dedicated to helping you manage your pain is just as important as clearly communicating the details of the pain you're experiencing to that healthcare provider. Be bold in your communication, write down questions before visiting the office, and don't leave until you're satisfied.

3 Keep A Positive Attitude—

Remain confident and upbeat about your condition, knowing that determination and commitment will play a large role in finding a solution to your pain.

Introduction: Getting Started

Common Conditions

Common Conditions II

Relieving Aches & Pains

Chronic Conditions

Medical Consumerism

Getting Active

Managing Weight

Introduction: Getting Started

Common Conditions

Common Conditions II

Relieving Aches & Pains

Chronic Conditions

Medical Consumerism

Getting Active

Managing Weight

DO YOU KNOW HOW TO CARE FOR...

Aches & Pains?

Take The Self-Care Quiz

The quiz below is designed to test your knowledge on the information presented in this section. Use this quiz as a tool to better understand how to care for yourself and others.

True   *False*

☐   ☐   **1)** Exercise, strength training, and weight control can help prevent back pain.

☐   ☐   **2)** Reducing stress, exercising regularly, quitting smoking, and avoiding headache "triggers" are strategies for preventing headaches.

☐   ☐   **3)** Leftovers should be refrigerated within four hours of eating.

☐   ☐   **4)** An individual is unhealthy if he or she doesn't have a daily bowel movement.

☐   ☐   **5)** Sudden, severe pain is always an emergency and reason to call 911.

Answers can be found inside this section.

Living with
Chronic Conditions

Cholesterol ★ High Blood Pressure ★ Heart Disease ★ Diabetes ★ Arthritis ★ Cancer ★ Asthma

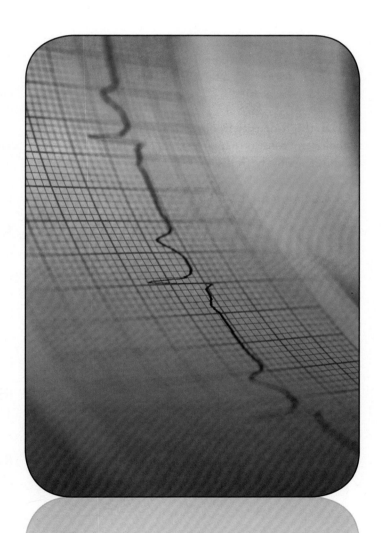

Self-Care **ESSENTIALS**®
A SIMPLE GUIDE TO MANAGING YOUR HEALTH CARE AND LIVING WELL

Understanding **Cholesterol**

About Cholesterol

Cholesterol is a soft, waxy substance found among the lipids (fats) in the bloodstream and in all of your body's cells. Although some cholesterol is an important part of a healthy body, a cholesterol level that's too high is a major risk factor for coronary heart disease, heart attack, and stroke.

There are two types of cholesterol—HDL (high-density lipoprotein) and LDL (low-density lipoprotein). These two combined equal your total cholesterol level. Triglycerides are also a factor to watch. Let's look at each in more detail.

HDL (high-density lipoprotein). This "good" cholesterol consists of high levels of protein that help protect against heart disease by carrying cholesterol away from the arteries. A level over 60 mg/dL is desirable (mg/dL stands for "milligrams per deciliter"—a measurement your healthcare provider will use).

LDL (low-density lipoprotein). LDL cholesterol is commonly referred to as "bad" cholesterol. We absorb bad cholesterol through fried, fatty foods. It has high levels of fat, but little protein, which makes it unstable, causing it to breakdown as it travels through the bloodstream. When LDL cholesterol breaks down, it is deposited on arterial walls, blocking blood flow to the heart. An LDL level below 100 mg/dL is desired and a level of 160 mg/dL or higher is considered high-risk.

Total cholesterol. Total cholesterol is the measure of both HDL and LDL combined. A total cholesterol level less than 200 mg/dL is desirable, and a level of 240 mg/dL or greater is considered high.

Triglycerides. Triglycerides are a form of fat. People with high levels of triglycerides often have high cholesterol and may be at high risk for coronary artery disease and stroke. Levels under 150 mg/dL are desired.

Signs & Symptoms

Symptoms

High cholesterol rarely causes symptoms. It is usually detected during a routine blood test performed by your healthcare provider. Cholesterol may first be discovered after a diagnosis of a condition caused in part by high cholesterol. These conditions may include stroke, coronary artery disease, etc.

Risk Factors

There are several risk factors for high cholesterol. Some risk factors are within your control, and others are not.

Risk Factors You Can Control
- ✓ Eating a high-fat, high-cholesterol diet
- ✓ Being overweight or obese
- ✓ Not exercising regularly
- ✓ Smoking

Risk Factors You Cannot Control
- ✓ Family History
- ✓ Age
- ✓ Gender

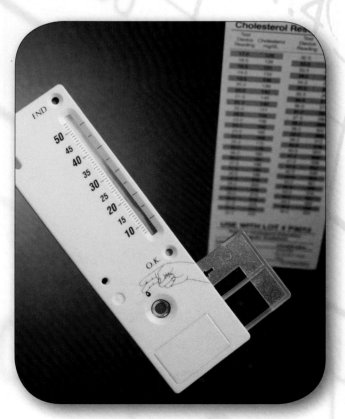

Introduction: Getting Started
Common Conditions
Common Conditions II
Relieving Aches & Pains
Chronic Conditions
Medical Consumerism
Getting Active
Managing Weight

A Self-Care Essential

Get Screened. Make a point of getting screened for high cholesterol regularly. If you're over the age of 20, you need to have your cholesterol checked every five years. High cholesterol can be managed—either with lifestyle modification, medication, or both—but you must know your cholesterol is high in order to address it effectively.

When To Seek Care

When considering high cholesterol, there are a number of situations in which you should seek medical help. Seek medical help in the following situations.

- If you're experiencing symptoms of a heart attack (refer to the section entitled, Heart Disease for more information) CALL 911!

- If you're over 20 and have not been screened (you should be screened for cholesterol every five years after age 20)

- If you think you may have diabetes (refer to the section entitled, Diabetes for more information)

- If you have a family history of high cholesterol, coronary artery disease, or diabetes

Managing Cholesterol

Home treatment for high cholesterol will include one of two strategies, and maybe both. These strategies include lifestyle modification and drug intervention.

Lifestyle Modification

⌂ **Reduce weight**—Losing weight can help reduce LDL cholesterol and raise HDL cholesterol.

⌂ **Exercise**—Moderate physical activity for 30 minutes most days of the week may help lower bad cholesterol and raise good cholesterol. Check with your healthcare provider before beginning an exercise program.

⌂ **Diet**—Diet changes may lower cholesterol as much as five to 20 percent.

⌂ **Quit smoking**—Studies have shown that HDL (good cholesterol) levels increase soon after quitting smoking.

Drug Intervention

If your total cholesterol, especially your LDL level, remains high despite lifestyle modifications, your healthcare provider may recommend drug intervention. Generally, an LDL level over 190, or an LDL over 160 with two or more risk factors, requires medication.

Blood Cholesterol Levels

Total Cholesterol Levels	Category
Less than 200 mg/dL	Desirable level that puts you at lower risk for coronary heart disease. A cholesterol level of 200 mg/dL or higher raises your risk.
200 to 239 mg/dL	Borderline high
240 mg/dL and above	High blood cholesterol. A person with this level has more than twice the risk of coronary heart disease as someone whose cholesterol is below 200 mg/dL.

HDL Cholesterol Levels	Category
Less than 40 mg/dL (men) Less than 50 mg/dL (women)	Low HDL cholesterol. A major risk factor for heart disease.
60 mg/dL and above	High HDL cholesterol. An HDL of 60 mg/dL and above is considered protective against heart disease.

If your total cholesterol is 200 mg/dL or more, or your HDL cholesterol is less than 40 mg/dL (for men) and less than 50 mg/dL (for women), you need to have a lipoprotein profile done to determine your LDL cholesterol and triglyceride levels. **If your cholesterol is high or you have other risk factors, your healthcare provider will likely want to monitor your cholesterol more closely.** Follow your provider's advice about how often to have your cholesterol tested. He or she will set appropriate management goals based on your LDL cholesterol level and other risk factors.

LDL Cholesterol Levels	Category
Less than 100 mg/dL	Optimal
100 to 129 mg/dL	Near or above optimal
130 to 159 mg/dL	Borderline high
160 to 189 mg/dL	High
190 mg/dL or above	Very high

Triglyceride Levels	Category
Less than 150 mg/dL	Normal
150 to 199 mg/dL	Borderline high
200 to 499 mg/dL	High
500 mg/dL or above	Very high

Source: American Heart Association Recommended Cholesterol Levels

Treating **High Blood Pressure**

Introduction: Getting Started

Common Conditions

Common Conditions II

Relieving Aches & Pains

Chronic Conditions

Medical Consumerism

Getting Active

Managing Weight

About High Blood Pressure

Blood pressure is the force of blood pushing against the walls of the arteries. When a person experiences high blood pressure (hypertension), the heart is forced to work harder than normal, causing it to grow abnormally large—straining arteries and the heart itself. High blood pressure can also damage kidneys and other organs, as well as lead to atherosclerosis (hardening of the arteries) and stroke.

A blood pressure reading consists of two numbers—systolic and diastolic. Let's look at each of these measurements in more detail.

Systolic—The systolic measurement is the pressure of blood against artery walls when the heart pumps blood through the body. It is the first number in a blood pressure reading, and is considered normal when it is less than 120 mmHg (mmHg means "millimeters of mercury"—a measure your healthcare provider will use in relation to blood pressure).

Diastolic—The diastolic measurement is the pressure of blood against the artery walls when the heart relaxes and refills with blood. It is the second number in a blood pressure reading, and it is considered normal when it is less than 80 mmHg.

> **Key Point:** A consistent reading of 120/80 mmHg or higher (the threshold of "prehypertension") is cause for discussion with your healthcare provider. See the chart in this section for a detailed break down of blood pressure levels.

Signs & Symptoms

Symptoms

High blood pressure is often called the "silent killer" because it has no symptoms. Sadly, it is estimated that of the 50 million Americans age six and over who have high blood pressure, one-third are unaware that they have the condition.

Risk Factors

Several risk factors—both controllable and uncontrollable—contribute to the likelihood of developing high blood pressure.

Risk Factors You Can Control

- ✓ Being overweight or obese
- ✓ Tobacco use
- ✓ Eating too much salt
- ✓ Consuming too much alcohol
- ✓ Living a sedentary lifestyle

Risk Factors You Cannot Control

- ✓ Race
- ✓ Age
- ✓ Family History

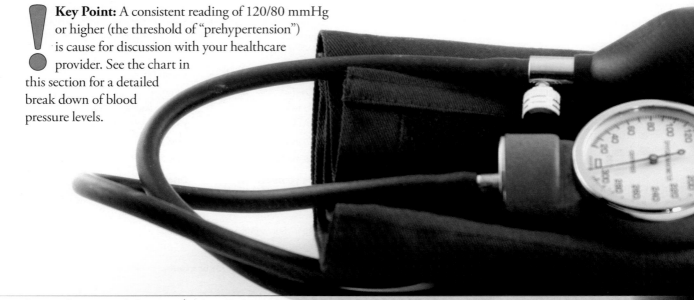

Introduction: Getting Started

Common Conditions

Common Conditions II

Relieving Aches & Pains

Chronic Conditions

Medical Consumerism

✚ A Self-Care Essential

Know Your Numbers. High blood pressure is often referred to as the "silent killer" because it has no symptoms. As with cholesterol and many other chronic conditions, it's important to get screened regularly. And, with the recent modification to blood pressure guidelines to include the category of "prehypertensive" it may be a good idea to get screened again soon. Many hospitals and community centers offer free screening services. Take advantage of these services and "know your numbers."

When To Seek Care

Call your healthcare provider immediately if you have high blood pressure and any of the following symptoms.

☤ If you're experiencing the symptoms of a heart attack (refer to the section entitled, ***Heart Disease*** for more information) CALL 911!

☤ If your blood pressure rises suddenly above a controlled, normal range

☤ If your blood pressure is 180/110 mmHg

☤ If you experience a sudden, severe headache

☤ If your blood pressure is higher than 140/90 mmHg on two or more separate occasions

☤ If you experience uncomfortable side effects that you believe are caused by blood pressure medication

Managing High Blood Pressure

Home treatment for high blood pressure will include one of two strategies, and maybe both. These strategies include lifestyle modification and drug intervention.

Lifestyle Modification

⌂ **Reduce weight**—Losing weight reduces the strain on your heart and will cause blood pressure to drop as a result.

⌂ **Exercise**—Lack of regular physical activity (30 minutes of moderate activity most days of the week) increases your risk for heart attack or stroke.

⌂ **Reduce alcohol intake**—Limit your alcohol consumption to no more than one or two drinks per day.

⌂ **Quit smoking**—Smoking is a major risk factor for almost every serious disease including high blood pressure.

⌂ **Alter your diet**—Eating a diet that's low in sodium may significantly reduce blood pressure.

Drug Intervention

Doctors have different opinions as to when medication is necessary; however, individuals with multiple risk factors for heart disease and elevated blood pressure (greater than 120/80 mmHg) are often treated using blood pressure medication in addition to lifestyle modification.

Source: American Heart Association

Blood Pressure Readings

Blood Pressure Classification	Systolic – mm Hg (upper #)		Diastolic – mm Hg (lower #)
Normal	less than 120	and	less than 80
Prehypertension	120-139	or	80-89
High Blood Pressure (Hypertension) Stage 1	140-159	or	90-99
High Blood Pressure (Hypertension) Stage 2	160 or higher	or	100 or higher
Hypertensive Crisis (Emergency care needed)	Higher than 180	or	Higher than 110

Source: American Heart Association Recommended Blood Pressure Levels. Content last reviewed on 04/04/2012.

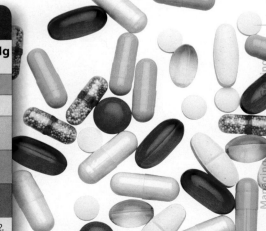

Understanding **Heart Disease**

Introduction: Getting Started

Common Conditions

Common Conditions II

Relieving Aches & Pains

Chronic Conditions

Medical Consumerism

Getting Active

Managing Weight

About Heart Disease

Your heart is a muscle that pumps blood to the organs and tissues in your body. This blood contains oxygen and nutrients to keep you alive, and it travels through a network of blood vessels that measures approximately 60,000 miles.

Although there are a number of conditions that can be classified as "heart disease," in this section, we'll concentrate on coronary artery disease—a heart condition in which fatty deposits clog and harden coronary arteries. This "hardening of the arteries" can typically occur in mid to late life, and blocks blood flow to your heart muscle. This blocked blood flow causes chest pain (angina) and, if the blood is blocked for a long enough period of time, a portion of the heart muscle can die. This is commonly known as a heart attack.

Because heart disease is the number one killer in the United States—and is also very preventable—it's important to know the symptoms and risk factors of heart disease.

Signs & Symptoms

Because heart disease tends to develop over a long period of time, symptoms can be vague, and may vary from person to person. Regardless, here are some tell tale signs that your heart may not be working correctly.

Symptoms

✓ Shortness of breath

✓ Pain in the chest (especially during exercise or hard work)

✓ Swelling in the legs

✓ Extreme fatigue

Risk Factors

✓ Family history of heart disease

✓ Poor nutrition

✓ Excessive stress

✓ Smoking

✓ Leading a sedentary lifestyle (lack of exercise)

✓ Being male

✓ Being overweight or obese

✓ Having high blood pressure, diabetes, or high cholesterol

"The network of blood vessels and arteries in the human body measures **approximately 60,000 miles**."

Introduction: Getting Started

Common Conditions

Common Conditions II

Relieving Aches & Pains

Chronic Conditions

Medical Consumerism

Getting Active

Managing Weight

A Self-Care Essential

Women and Heart Disease. Heart disease is not just a man's disease! In fact, heart disease is actually the leading cause of death among American women today. 267,000 women die each year from heart attacks (six times more than the number that die from breast cancer). The good news is that by working with your healthcare provider to get regular screenings and checkups, you can address your risk factors before it's too late. Schedule an appointment today.

When To Seek Care

The symptoms of heart disease should clue you in that your heart is not functioning properly. If you are experiencing any of the symptoms of heart disease outlined in this section, you should contact your healthcare provider who can screen you for the presence of heart disease and help you implement an action plan.

Heart disease in advanced stages can lead to a heart attack, meaning that blood flow to a coronary artery is blocked for a significant amount of time (approximately 30 minutes to 2 hours). If this happens, you'll experience what is commonly known as a heart attack. A heart attack is a life-threatening event. Call 911 immediately if you're experiencing any of the following symptoms.

Symptoms of a Heart Attack

- If there is burning, crushing, and/or squeezing pain or pressure in the chest

- If there is pain in the arms, neck, back, and/or jaw

- If pain doesn't go away or lasts longer than 15 minutes

- If you experience an irregular pulse or heartbeat

- If you experience nausea, vomiting, shortness of breath, dizziness, weakness, or sweating

Managing Heart Disease

Heart disease is a serious condition that requires the attention of a healthcare provider. You and your healthcare provider can establish a plan of action for managing your condition most effectively. Make sure to include the following steps in your action plan.

⌂ **Take prescribed medications as directed.** Medications can be an important part of managing heart disease.

⌂ **Quit smoking.** Quitting smoking may be the best decision to improve your health—period.

⌂ **Exercise regularly.** Check with your healthcare provider before beginning an exercise program.

⌂ **Eat a diet low in cholesterol.** Eat more pasta, whole grains, etc.

⌂ **Control high blood pressure.** High blood pressure can be controlled through medication or lifestyle changes.

⌂ **Reduce stress.** Try meditation, deep breathing, guided imagery, etc.

⌂ **Lose weight.** Eating sensibly can help you maintain a proper weight.

⌂ **Speak with your healthcare provider about aspirin use.** According to the American Heart Association, aspirin helps prevent the recurrence of heart attacks.

Treating **Diabetes**

About Diabetes

Diabetes is a serious disease. If not diagnosed and treated early, it can result in blindness, heart attack, stroke, kidney failure, birth defects, and limb loss. What's more, diabetes kills approximately 200,000 people each year.

Startlingly, you may not know you have it. Onset is often gradual and difficult to identify—you can have diabetes without any symptoms. In fact, half of those affected don't even know they have the disease until they seek help for one of its complications. Diabetes is a growing disease—800,000 new cases of diabetes are diagnosed each year—a number that is expected to rise as baby boomers age.

There are two main types of diabetes—type 1 and type 2. Both are caused by the body's inability to produce or properly use insulin—a hormone that maintains the proper level of sugar in your blood.

Type 1 Diabetes: Type 1 diabetes is often diagnosed in children and young adults, and may have a sudden and severe onset, requiring emergency medical care. The body's immune system attacks and destroys the ability of the pancreas to make insulin, so people with type 1 diabetes must eat a special diet, get

A glucometer is often used by diabetics to check blood sugar levels.

regular exercise, check their blood sugar levels, and give themselves shots of insulin several times throughout the day.

Type 2 Diabetes: Ninety to 95 percent of people with diabetes have type 2. It is usually diagnosed in older adults, although overweight children sometimes develop it as well. It is caused by the pancreas not making enough insulin, or the body not using it well. People can have type 2 diabetes for years without symptoms, yet it is still damaging to their bodies.

Signs & Symptoms

The symptoms of diabetes may be hard to recognize, and are sometimes mistaken for signs of aging. The risk factors for diabetes, however, are straightforward.

Symptoms:
✓ Increased thirst

✓ Extreme hunger

✓ Frequent urination

✓ Unexplained weight loss

✓ Fatigue, dizziness, and weakness

✓ Trouble seeing or blurred vision

✓ Sores that heal slowly

✓ Recurring infections of the skin, bladder, and vagina

Risk Factors:
✓ Being 45 years of age or older

✓ A family history of diabetes

✓ Being overweight or obese

✓ Having high blood pressure—140/90 mmHg or higher

✓ Leading a sedentary lifestyle

✓ Being a Native American, African American, Asian American, or Pacific Islander

✓ Having a baby weighing more than nine pounds at birth

A Self-Care Essential

Weighty Matters. According to the American Diabetes Association, nearly 90 percent of all people with newly diagnosed type 2 diabetes are overweight. And with about 60 percent of Americans now overweight or obese, it's no surprise that 800,000 new cases of diabetes are reported each year. But remember, it is possible to lose weight and keep it off. Talk with your healthcare provider to develop a strategy that's right for you.

When To Seek Care

Diabetes is a serious condition that requires the regular attention of a healthcare provider. With that in mind, seek immediate emergency care in the following situations.

- If a known diabetic is unconscious
- If you or a loved one is exhibiting the classic signs of diabetes (increased thirst, extreme hunger, frequent urination, etc.)
- If blood sugar drops and cannot be restored within fifteen minutes after ingesting a sugary substance
- If a diabetic is unable to eat or is vomiting
- If a known diabetic suspects she is pregnant

Managing Diabetes

There is no cure for diabetes yet, but there is much you can do to manage the disease. Include the following in your diabetes management plan.

- ⌂ **Monitor blood sugar levels.**
- ⌂ **Take insulin and other medications as directed.**
- ⌂ **Manage your weight.**
- ⌂ **Eat small, regular meals that include lots of fiber** (fruits, vegetables, and whole grains).
- ⌂ **Exercise regularly** (moderate exercise for 30 minutes most days of the week—check with your healthcare provider before beginning an exercise program).
- ⌂ **Communicate regularly with your healthcare professional.**
- ⌂ **Have your eyes and feet checked by a healthcare provider every year** and closely monitor blood pressure and cholesterol levels.
- ⌂ **Be cautious if drinking alcohol** (check blood sugar levels as needed, and make sure to eat either before or while you drink).

Common Conditions

Common Conditions II

Relieving Aches & Pains

Chronic Conditions

Medical Consumerism

Getting Active

Understanding **Arthritis**

About Arthritis

Arthritis is a chronic condition that can cause a great deal of pain and severely limit an individual's activities. Arthritis is much more common in older adults, but the perception that the disease is a condition that only affects older adults is off base. In fact, most people with arthritis are younger than 65, and nearly 300,000 children are affected by arthritis as well.

Arthritis is a disease of the joints, and causes the membranes, cartilage, and tissues around the joints to become inflamed. After prolonged inflammation and breakdown, joints can become severely damaged, causing permanent disability.

At this time, the cause of arthritis is not known; although researchers are investigating the possibility that a virus may cause the body's immune system to attack the joints. There is no cure for arthritis; however, it can be effectively managed using self-care techniques.

Signs & Symptoms

There are more than 100 different types of arthritis. Osteoarthritis, rheumatoid arthritis, and gout are the most common forms. Osteoarthritis causes cartilage to break down resulting in bones rubbing together. Rheumatoid arthritis causes the tissues lining the joints to become inflamed leading to disability. Gout is a disease caused by the deposit of uric acid crystals in the joints. The symptoms of these three common forms of arthritis include the following.

Symptoms

✓ Pain or stiffness of joints (especially in the knees, fingers, hips, and feet)

✓ Swelling of joints

✓ Sudden and strong pain

✓ General stiffness in the mornings, or after prolonged rest

✓ Redness or heat surrounding a joint

Risk Factors

✓ A possible genetic predisposition to arthritis

✓ Being female

✓ Being between the ages of 50 and 70

✓ Having experienced an injury to a joint

✓ Long-term wear and tear on joints

Introduction: Getting Started

Common Conditions

Common Conditions II

Relieving Aches & Pains

Chronic Conditions

Medical Consumerism

Getting Active

Managing Weight

"Nearly **70 million Americans** have arthritis or chronic joint symptoms. As the population ages, this number will probably increase dramatically."

A Self-Care Essential

What About Arthritis-Specific Diets? While there are several "arthritis-specific" diets that claim to reduce arthritis symptoms—or even cure the condition—the Arthritis Foundation recommends arthritis sufferers evaluate unproven diets very carefully. Arthritis-specific diets known to have harmful side effects are those that rely on heavy doses of alfalfa, copper salts or zinc, or the so-called immune power diet or the low-calorie/low-fat/low-protein diet. The Arthritis Foundation recommends a sensible diet that includes variety, balance, and moderation to help arthritis sufferers maintain a healthy weight and potentially reduce symptoms.

When To Seek Care

Because arthritis can be a serious chronic condition, it's important that you involve your healthcare provider in the decision making process. You'll especially want to call your healthcare provider if you exhibit any of the following symptoms.

⚕ If pain and swelling in and surrounding the joints comes on suddenly with no explanation

⚕ If joint pain is associated with fever or rash

⚕ If the joint is so inflamed and painful that it's impossible to use

⚕ If your pain does not improve after six weeks of self-care

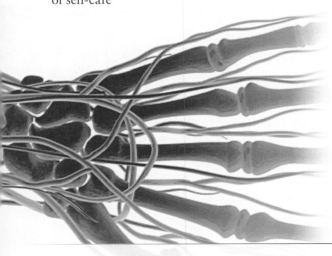

Managing Arthritis

There are many steps you can take to treat arthritis in the comfort of your own home. Here's a list of some helpful self-care strategies.

⌂ **Use ice**—Apply ice or cold packs to reduce pain and swelling.

⌂ **Get rest**—Get plenty of rest and talk with your healthcare provider about the best sleeping position for you.

⌂ **Take your meds**—Take any medications prescribed by your doctor according to directions. Be careful of drug interactions.

⌂ **Use self-care**—Take over-the-counter medications such as ibuprofen or acetaminophen to relieve pain. Be careful of drug interactions. Do not give aspirin to children.

⌂ **Warm up**—Take a warm shower or bath to loosen and relax stiff, swollen joints. Heat is often very helpful in relaxing and soothing sore muscles and joints.

⌂ **Keep moving**—Keep active to prevent joints from becoming stiff. Often, prolonged rest can further irritate arthritis. You should be able to move without significant pain.

⌂ **Try low-impact exercises**—When exercising, try low-impact exercises like swimming that won't irritate your arthritis. Check with your healthcare provider before beginning an exercise program.

⌂ **Keep stretching**—Stretch your joints and muscles daily, taking them through their full range of motion. This will help to keep your joints and muscles more limber.

⌂ **Learn more**—Educate yourself and others about your condition. Try visiting the Arthritis Foundation at **www.arthritis.org**.

⌂ **Stay positive**—Stay positive about your condition. Even though there's currently not a cure, there are many ways to manage arthritis.

Introduction: Getting Started

Common Conditions

Common Conditions II

Relieving Aches & Pains

Chronic Conditions

Medical Consumerism

Getting Active

Managing Weight

Understanding **Cancer**

Introduction: Getting Started
Common Conditions
Common Conditions II
Relieving Aches & Pains
Chronic Conditions
Medical Consumerism
Getting Active
Managing Weight

About Cancer

Cancer is caused when cells in a part of the body begin to grow out of control. Although there are many types of cancer, they all start because of the out-of-control growth of abnormal cells.

In healthy adults, normal cells only divide and multiply to replace dead or injured cells. Abnormal cells are different from normal cells because they continue to grow and divide. This out-of-control growth can lead to the formation of masses (tumors)—which may or may not be cancerous.

Signs & Symptoms

Because cancer can take many forms, and affect many parts of the body, the signs and symptoms of cancer are numerous. Often times, the signs and symptoms of cancer depend on the type and location of the cancer. Additionally, because the general signs and symptoms

of cancer may often mimic the symptoms of other conditions, it's important to follow regular cancer screening schedules—see the chart on the following page. Listed here are some of the general, as well as specific signs and symptoms of cancer.

General Signs and Symptoms of Cancer

✓ Unexplained weight loss   ✓ Pain

✓ Fever   ✓ Skin changes

✓ Fatigue

Specific Signs and Symptoms of Cancer

✓ Changes in bowel habits or bladder function (colon, bladder, or prostate cancer)

✓ Sores that do not heal or recent changes in a wart or mole (skin cancer)

✓ Unusual bleeding or discharge (lung, cervical, bladder, or kidney cancer)

✓ Thickening or a lump in the breast, testicle, or other part of the body (breast or testicular cancer)

✓ Indigestion, difficulty swallowing, nagging cough, or hoarseness (stomach, esophagus, or throat cancer)

If you're experiencing any of the above signs and symptoms of cancer, it's important to see your healthcare provider right away. Early detection is one of the most important variables in successful cancer treatment.

Risk Factors For Cancer

There are a number of risk factors for developing cancer. Some of these risk factors are within your control, and others are not.

Risk Factors You Can Control

✓ Smoking and tobacco use   ✓ Sun exposure

✓ Being overweight or obese   ✓ Radon exposure

✓ Not exercising regularly

Risk Factors You Cannot Control

✓ Family history

✓ Age

✓ Gender

> "Some forms of cancer are thought to be **hereditary**, making **family health history** an important risk factor."

✚ A Self-Care Essential

It's Never Too Late to Quit Smoking. No matter what your age or how long you've smoked, quitting will help you live longer. Statistics prove that smokers are twice as likely to die from heart attacks as are non-smokers. But quitting smoking now greatly reduces your chances of developing serious health problems. According to the American Lung Association, people who quit smoking before the age of 35 avoid 90 percent of the health risks attributable to tobacco use. Those who quit smoking before age 50 have one-half the risk of dying in the next 15 years compared with continuing smokers. Kick the habit!

Cancer Screening Guidelines

The American Cancer Society recommends that all adults get these regular cancer screening tests, so that cancer can be discovered and treated early. People with increased risk for cancer may need more frequent and additional tests.

Test	Gender	Age	Frequency
Doctor exam for cancer	Men/ Women	20 and over	Annually with Health Exam
Sigmoidoscopy	Men/ Women	50 and over	Every 5 years
Testicular self-exam	Men	20 and over	Optional
Prostate-specific antigen	Men	50 and over	Annually
Breast self-exam	Women	20 and over	Optional
Doctor breast exam	Women	20 to 39	Every 3 years
		40 and over	Annually
Mammogram	Women	40 and over	Annually
Pelvic exam	Women	Not Specified	Discuss with Healthcare Provider
Pap smear*	Women	18 and over or three years after starting vaginal intercourse	Annually

*After three or more consecutive satisfactory examinations with normal findings, the Pap smear test may be performed less frequently at the doctor's discretion.

Note: Health screening guidelines may change regularly. Be sure to check with your healthcare provider on the screenings that are appropriate for you.

When To Seek Care

If you're experiencing any of the signs and symptoms of cancer listed in this section, it's important to see your healthcare provider right away. Moreover, because early detection is one of the most important variables in successful cancer treatment, it's important to follow the cancer screening guidelines outlined in this section.

Managing Cancer

Cancer is a serious health condition and treatment will be a decision made between you and your healthcare team. Whatever course of treatment you choose, there are some things you can do to help better manage cancer throughout the treatment process and beyond.

Respond Appropriately To Your Diagnosis

Learning as much as you can about your condition, communicating openly with loved ones, keeping a positive attitude, and learning about your insurance coverage can go a long way toward helping you cope with a cancer diagnosis.

Watch Your Nutrition

Cancer often disrupts the body's ability to absorb important nutrients, and can also lessen one's appetite. Therefore, it's important to make a registered dietician a part of your healthcare team.

Control Pain

Here's encouraging news—more than half of all cancer patients do not experience significant pain. If pain exists, it can almost always be managed. Over-the-counter pain relievers can be very effective, and narcotics and tranquilizers exist for severe pain. Talk with your healthcare provider about the right pain management strategy for you.

Source: American Cancer Society

Introduction: Getting Started

Common Conditions

Common Conditions II

Relieving Aches & Pains

Chronic Conditions

Medical Consumerism

Getting Active

Managing Weight

Understanding **Asthma**

Introduction: Getting Started

Common Conditions

Common Conditions II

Relieving Aches & Pains

Chronic Conditions

Medical Consumerism

Getting Active

Managing Weight

About Asthma

Asthma is a chronic disease that affects a person's airways—the tubes that carry air in and out of the lungs. Asthma causes the inside walls of the airways to become inflamed. This inflammation makes the airways very sensitive, and they tend to react strongly to "triggers"—things to which you are allergic or find irritating.

When these airways react, they get narrower and less air flows to the lungs. This causes symptoms like wheezing (a whistling sound when you breathe), coughing, chest tightness, and trouble breathing.

"Asthma 'triggers' include things like **tobacco smoke, pet dander, dust**, and **pollen**."

Signs & Symptoms

Common asthma symptoms include:

✓ Coughing
✓ Chest tightness
✓ Faster or noisy breathing
✓ Wheezing
✓ Shortness of breath

People with asthma may have:

✓ Symptoms brought on by exercises such as running, biking, or other brisk activity, especially during cold weather

✓ Coughing or wheezing brought on by prolonged crying or laughing

✓ Coughing or wheezing when near an allergen or irritant like tobacco smoke, pet dander, dust, or pollen

Risk Factors

Although there are a number of "triggers"—like tobacco smoke, pet dander, dust, or pollen—which may further irritate a person's asthma, or even incite an asthma attack, risk factors for asthma are largely beyond our control. Risk factors include the following.

✓ **Age**—Although asthma affects people of all ages, it often starts in childhood and is more common in children than adults.

✓ **Allergies**—Asthma is closely linked to allergies. In fact, most people with asthma have allergies.

✓ **Gender**—More boys have asthma than girls, but in adulthood, more women have asthma than men.

✓ **Family history**—Individuals who inherit a tendency toward overreactive bronchial tubes may be more likely to develop asthma.

✓ **Race**—Although asthma is a problem among all races, African Americans have more asthma attacks and are more likely than whites to be hospitalized for asthma attacks and to die from asthma.

A Self-Care Essential

Stress and Asthma. According to the American Academy of Allergies, Asthma, and Immunology, stress can lower your immune system's ability to manage chronic conditions such as asthma. People with asthma may be more likely to get sick if under a high degree of stress.

If you're an asthma sufferer, try implementing the following stress management strategies to strengthen your body's ability to manage your asthma better.

- Avoid stressful situations
- Practice relaxation techniques
- Get plenty of exercise
- Eat well
- Get plenty of sleep
- Develop a strong, social support network

When To Seek Care

Most of the time, asthma can easily be managed in the comfort of your own home. There are, however, times when your asthma may need immediate medical attention. Call 911 immediately in the following situations.

- If you have severe difficulty breathing

- If breathing doesn't become easier 20 minutes after taking your medication

"See a doctor if you have **severe difficulty** breathing or if breathing doesn't become easier **20 minutes after taking your medication.**"

Managing Asthma

If you have asthma, it is important to learn how to take care of yourself. The following tips and strategies will prove helpful if you or a loved one is dealing with asthma.

- **Develop an "asthma action plan" with your healthcare provider.** This involves using a peak-flow meter to gauge how well you're breathing, and to determine the best course of treatment for individual asthma incidents.

- **Become familiar with the substances that "trigger" your asthma, and avoid them.** Often these "triggers" include tobacco smoke, pet dander, dust, or pollen.

- **Drink extra fluids to help thin and clear mucus** from the bronchial tubes.

- **Learn to use your medication correctly.** Ask your doctor about using an inhaler—a device used to deliver metered doses of medicine to the lungs.

- **Consider keeping a diary to record details about your asthma attacks** so you can better avoid them in the future.

- **Communicate regularly with your healthcare provider** about your condition.

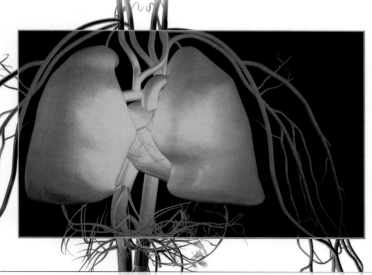

Introduction, Getting Started

Common Conditions

Common Conditions II

Relieving Aches & Pains

Chronic Conditions

Medical Consumerism

Getting Active

Managing Weight

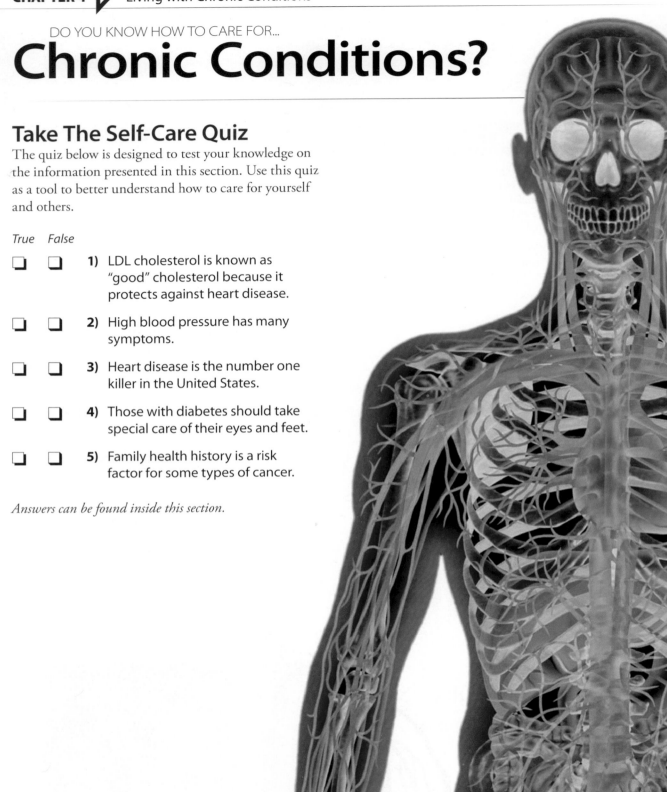

DO YOU KNOW HOW TO CARE FOR...

Chronic Conditions?

Take The Self-Care Quiz

The quiz below is designed to test your knowledge on the information presented in this section. Use this quiz as a tool to better understand how to care for yourself and others.

True   False

☐   ☐   **1)** LDL cholesterol is known as "good" cholesterol because it protects against heart disease.

☐   ☐   **2)** High blood pressure has many symptoms.

☐   ☐   **3)** Heart disease is the number one killer in the United States.

☐   ☐   **4)** Those with diabetes should take special care of their eyes and feet.

☐   ☐   **5)** Family health history is a risk factor for some types of cancer.

Answers can be found inside this section.

Introduction: Getting Started

Common Conditions

Common Conditions II

Relieving Aches & Pains

Chronic Conditions

Medical Consumerism

Getting Active

Managing Weight

A Guide To
Medical Consumerism

Your Healthcare Provider ★ Preventive Screenings ★ Managing Your Medications
Preventing Medical Errors ★ About Health Risk Appraisals

Self-Care ESSENTIALS®
A SIMPLE GUIDE TO MANAGING YOUR HEALTH CARE AND LIVING WELL

Your **Healthcare Provider**

Introduction: Getting Started

Common Conditions

Common Conditions II

Relieving Aches & Pains

Chronic Conditions

Medical Consumerism

Getting Active

Managing Weight

Getting The Most From Your Visit To The Healthcare Provider

If your condition is serious enough that it warrants a visit to your healthcare provider, you're going to need to be prepared. Too many of us visit our healthcare providers, and simply nod our heads through the entire visit, leaving with more questions than we had when we arrived. If you are to become a wise consumer of healthcare, you're going to need to know how to make the most of your visit to your healthcare provider.

Thankfully, following a few simple guidelines can go a long way toward ensuring that you not only get the care you need, but that you also leave the office with your questions answered—feeling good about your recommended course of treatment.

Take a look at the following guidelines for getting the most from your visit to the healthcare provider.

Before Your Visit
Decide What You Want

Decide what you want from your healthcare provider before you step foot in the office. Are you looking for a diagnosis? Do you need reassurance about your condition? Are you seeking information about new developments on your condition? Decide what you want before your visit, and don't leave until you get it.

Make A List

After you decide what you want from the visit, write it down! You will probably have several goals for the visit, so prioritize your list and ask your most important questions first. Don't forget to review the list with friends or loved ones familiar with your condition—they may come up with some good questions you forgot to list.

Practice

It may sound silly, but practicing your questions before you get into the office can help you better articulate your goals when it comes time to visit with your healthcare provider. And, because physicians' offices can be intimidating, rehearsing your questions will make them easier to ask because you'll know exactly what you need to say. Don't be embarrassed—practice your questions, even if it's in the car on the way to the office.

Gather The Necessary Information

Get all of your health-related information in order before you visit your healthcare provider. Make sure to gather information on the medications you may be taking (names and recommended dosages), symptoms, any previous or current lifestyle treatments/changes, and any relevant test results. Gathering this info beforehand can save you time and energy, and may even help you feel better faster.

"**Taking part in decisions** about your care is an important part of being a wise healthcare consume

During Your Visit

Ask Your Questions with Confidence

Tell your healthcare provider right away that you have a list of things to discuss. You've put in all the work to prepare for the visit, now it's time to be bold. It's not uncommon for some patients to clam up once they're in the office, but don't let it happen to you. Be bold with your questions, and if you are unclear about the answer, ask for an explanation. Don't be intimidated or feel like you're taking too much of your healthcare provider's time. Your health is the most important thing you have. You absolutely must get proper care, have your questions answered satisfactorily, and feel confident in your course of treatment after the visit. This is a "non-negotiable."

Take Part In Decisions About Your Care

Healthcare providers spend their days deciding how to best deliver care to patients. Often, they get little input from the patient during the process. This ironic fact of modern medicine can lead to treatment goals that aren't right for you or your lifestyle. Again, it comes down to what you—the consumer—want from your visit. Are you looking for aggressive treatment, or an easy way to manage your condition? How do you feel about new procedures? What would increase your quality of life the most? Keep these and other questions in mind when taking part in decisions about your care.

Ask Your Healthcare Provider To Sum Up Before He/She Leaves The Room

In some cases, a good conversation with your healthcare provider may lead to discussions outside the realm of care. And while it's good to get some details and insight into your condition, you need to leave the office with key points for moving forward. To make sure this happens, ask your healthcare provider to sum up the visit in a few key bullet points. You may want to ask, "What are the most important things I need to remember after I leave?"

It's a good idea to write down these main points on a small tablet while you're still in the office. Don't feel like writing the points down? You should—a recent study found that patients forget 80 percent of what the doctor told them as soon as they leave the office. Worse yet, half of what is remembered is remembered incorrectly.

Ask For Resources

Your healthcare provider's office is full of resources to help you better understand your condition. Make sure to ask for a pamphlet covering your condition, so you can further educate yourself on proper care. Your healthcare provider may also know of other reliable information in print or electronic format that you can access outside of the office for little or no cost. In the information age, make sure to get information on the topics that matter most to you.

Continued on the following page...

Introduction: Getting Started

Common Conditions

Common Conditions II

Relieving Aches & Pains

Chronic Conditions

Medical Consumerism

Getting Active

Your **Healthcare Provider**

Continued...

(sidebar tabs:) Introduction: Getting Started | Common Conditions | Common Conditions II | Relieving Aches & Pains | Chronic Conditions | **Medical Consumerism** | Getting Active | Managing Weight

After Your Visit

Review Your Appointment

Review the appointment in your mind after leaving the healthcare provider's office. Consider the main points you discussed, as well as your treatment plan and any other important information. Once you arrive home, look at your notes again to make sure you didn't forget anything vital. File your list in a safe place (perhaps with your first aid kit) so you can refer to it quickly and easily. You should be able to recite the main points of treatment before you put your list away.

Involve Your Pharmacist

The pharmacist is an important link in the healthcare chain. If you have been prescribed medication for your condition, use the pharmacist as a resource. Ask him/her about the medication you've been prescribed. How common is it for your condition? Are there side effects? What should you do if you miss a dose? Don't forget to ask about getting a generic substitute! Generics can be just as effective and may cost substantially less. You may even reduce your co-pay.

Pick Up The Phone If Necessary

If you feel unsure about your treatment, or can't remember important specifics, don't hesitate to call your healthcare provider's office. You have the right to get the best care possible, and besides, your healthcare provider would rather get a phone call than hear that you've treated yourself incorrectly. Remember, studies show that patients who don't understand treatment orders make more medication errors, comply with treatment less often, and are more likely to suffer from long-term untreated illnesses.

Take Control of Your Health

In the end, it comes down to taking a different perspective on future visits to your healthcare provider. Instead of sitting quietly, nodding your way through the appointment, and dealing with uncertainty after you leave, start taking more control—and more interest—in your health and your healthcare.

Write down important questions, practice asking them before your visit, and voice them boldly once you arrive at the office. Make sure you're well prepared for your appointment by gathering information about your medical history before the visit, and then take part in decisions about your care. Ask your healthcare provider to sum up main points before he/she leaves the room, review your treatment plan, and involve your pharmacist in the process when appropriate. Following the steps listed here will ensure that you get the most out of your visit to the healthcare provider, and your health.

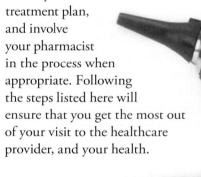

5 Important Questions To Ask

Don't leave your healthcare provider's office without having definitive answers to the following questions. Knowing the answers will be helpful during the treatment process, and will better ensure the safety of you and your loved ones.

1. What are the most important things I need to remember when I leave the office?

2. Why have you recommended this course of treatment?

3. Are there alternatives to the recommended course of treatment? If so, what are they?

4. What can I do to reduce my health risks in the future?

5. If I have additional questions, how will I get them answered in a timely manner?

"**Write down** important questions, **practice asking** them before your visit, and **voice them boldly** once you arrive at the office."

Preventive **Screenings**

Introduction: Getting Started

Common Conditions

Common Conditions II

Relieving Aches & Pains

Chronic Conditions

Medical Consumerism

Getting Active

Managing Weight

About Screenings

Regular health exams and screenings are important because they can help to identify potential health problems in the early stages, when they may be easier to treat. Preventive health screenings may also act as a springboard for you and your healthcare provider to develop an action plan to address current health challenges and to prevent new problems from occurring in the future.

Getting regular health screenings and checkups is a fundamental part of being a savvy healthcare consumer. Your health, ultimately, is not your healthcare provider's responsibility, but your own—and paying attention to important health screenings is one of the most important things you can do to live a long and vital life.

Included here, you'll find screening forms, as well as screening guidelines for both men and women. Read this information carefully, and be sure you make regular preventive screenings a part of your healthcare regimen.

MEN'S SCREENING FORM

Take this form with you to your healthcare provider's office and fill it out when you have had any of the tests listed below. Talk to your healthcare provider about when these tests should be performed, and note the month and year in the right-hand column. Also, talk to your healthcare provider about which of the other tests listed below you should have in the future, and when you need them.

Test	The Last Time I Had The Following Screening Test Was: (mm/yy)	I Should Schedule My Next Screening Test For: (mm/yy)
Cholesterol		
Blood Pressure		
Colorectal Cancer		
Sexually Transmitted Disease		
Prostate Cancer		

WOMEN'S SCREENING FORM

Take this form with you to your healthcare provider's office and fill it out when you have had any of the tests listed below. Talk to your healthcare provider about when these tests should be performed, and note the month and year in the right-hand column. Also, talk to your healthcare provider about which of the other tests listed below you should have in the future, and when you need them.

Test	The Last Time I Had The Following Screening Test Was: (mm/yy)	I Should Schedule My Next Screening Test For: (mm/yy)
Mammogram		
Pap Smear		
Cholesterol		
Blood Pressure		
Colorectal Cancer		
Osteoporosis		
Chlamydia and other STDs		

Download Your Guide
to Clinical Preventive Services at
www.ahrq.gov/clinic/pocketgd.htm

Note: Web addresses change frequently. To access the Agency for Healthcare Research and Quality's website, log on to **www.ahrq.gov** for the most recent information.

The Guide to Clinical Preventive Services 2010 - 2011

Recommendations of the U.S. Preventive Services Task Force

AHRQ
Agency for Healthcare Research and Quality
Advancing Excellence in Health Care

USPSTF

Introduction: Getting Started

Common Conditions

Common Conditions II.

Relieving Aches & Pains

Chronic Conditions

Medical Consumerism

Getting Active

Managing Weight

Managing **Your Medications**

Introduction: Getting Started

Common Conditions

Common Conditions II

Relieving Aches & Pains

Chronic Conditions

Medical Consumerism

Getting Active

Managing Weight

About Managing Your Medications

Medications are a significant part of our lives as medical consumers. In fact, 46 percent of the total population uses prescription medications in any given year, and 84 percent of consumers use over-the-counter (OTC) medications each year. While medications can be extremely helpful in treating medical conditions, it's important to understand them so that you can maximize their effectiveness and protect your health.

Understanding Your Medicines

Each year, thousands of people are hospitalized, remain sick, and spend more money than they have to because they don't understand their medications. The American Pharmacists Association recommends that you be able to answer the following ten key questions before taking any new medications.

Ten Key Medication Questions

1. What is the name of the medication and what is it supposed to do?

2. When and how do I take it?

3. How long should I take it?

4. Does this medication contain anything that can cause an allergic reaction?

5. Should I avoid alcohol, any other medicines, food, and/or activities?

6. Should I expect any side effects?

7. What if I forget to take my medication?

8. Is it safe to become pregnant or to breast-feed while taking this medication?

9. Is there a generic version of this medication?

10. How should this medication be stored?

Making Medications Work Better

Modern medicine has brought about countless medications to help us feel better fast. But there are still things you can do to ensure that your medications work for you. Keep three words in mind: dosage, generics, and compliance.

Dosage

Specific dosages are prescribed for a reason. Never modify your dosage (i.e., break pills in half or otherwise change your dosage) without first talking with your healthcare provider and pharmacist! Not only can this can be dangerous, but it can also delay healing.

Generic Medications

Brand-name medications can be extremely expensive. In fact, Americans spend about $100 billion on prescription drugs every year. Many times, there's no need to spend so much for prescriptions. Generic drugs are those drugs that have been judged chemically equivalent to brand-name drugs by the FDA. If it's available and appropriate, you may want to consider choosing a generic equivalent.

Compliance

Compliance means taking your medication as prescribed by your doctor and pharmacist. Skipping dosages or not finishing medication is not recommended. Drugs have little benefit if not taken as directed. If you're skipping dosages or "saving medication," consider this: you'll probably spend more money in the long-run treating the same disease twice, or addressing complications that arise from not being compliant.

"Americans spend about **100 billion** on prescription drugs every year."

How To Get The Most From Your Pharmacist

Your pharmacist is an important part of your healthcare decision making team. This trained medical professional does much more than count tablets and pour liquids. In fact, they can do much to increase the quality of your healthcare.

The following strategies will help you get the most from your pharmacist, ultimately increasing your health and well-being in the short- and long-term.

Pick a permanent pharmacist/pharmacy

By always going to the same pharmacy or pharmacist, you'll better ensure that your medical records are on file and at hand—helping you avoid complications and potential drug interactions. Not only will choosing a single pharmacy or pharmacist protect your health, but it can also save you headaches and worry as you'll only have to collect important health-related documents one time.

Involve your pharmacist in your OTC decisions

Pharmaceutical drugs are not the only medications you'll take—in fact, it's likely that you'll purchase more over-the-counter medications during your lifetime. Make sure to check with your pharmacist on OTC medications you are unsure about. With many pharmacies now located in supermarkets and other convenient locations where you purchase OTC medications, involving your pharmacist in your OTC decisions becomes easier than ever.

Develop a relationship with your pharmacist

Getting the most from your pharmacist means getting to know him or her, and allowing them to learn a little bit about you as well. Share with your pharmacist any financial concerns about the cost of drugs, family history, and any personal health goals you'd like to achieve. By doing so, your pharmacist may be more likely to offer important insight and advice that will help you become a wise healthcare consumer.

Continued on the following page...

Introduction: Getting Started

Common Conditions

Common Conditions II

Relieving Aches & Pains

Chronic Conditions

Medical Consumerism

Getting Active

Managing Weight

Managing **Your Medications**

Continued...

Avoiding Medication Errors

Each year, more than 770,000 Americans are injured because of medication errors. It has also been estimated that medication errors account for at least 7,000 deaths annually. Without a doubt, taking medications is serious business for you and your family.

Unfortunately, many of us become complacent or have a false sense of security about some of the powerful over-the-counter and prescription medications we take on a regular basis. And while there's no need to be fearful of medications, there are some simple ground rules to follow to help ensure your safety and health. Keep the following in mind when taking medications.

✓ **Know your medications inside and out.** Make a list of all the medications you are taking along with the dosage, color, shape, size, and imprint on the pill. Knowing this information will help you recognize medications that may have been given to you by mistake.

✓ **Keep medications in their original containers.** The label on your medication bottle contains important information about how the medicine inside is to be used. If you switch medications to another container, you're asking for trouble and could be putting your health in serious jeopardy.

✓ **Read, read, read.** Every time you take your medications, read the label on the container. Although it may be monotonous, doing so will help ensure that you take the right medication, at the right time, and in the right dosage—every time.

✓ **Turn on the light.** Never take medications in the dark (for instance, getting up in the middle of the night to take a pill). It's hard to distinguish between pills, and it can be easy to grab the wrong bottle in the dark—especially when you're half asleep.

✓ **Only take medication prescribed for you.** Never take another person's medication—not even medication prescribed to a family member. Medications are prescribed specifically for individuals based on their unique requirements.

✓ **Comply with medication directions.** Do not break pills or alter dosages. Don't skip dosages or stop taking medications early. Follow directions carefully.

YOUR MEDICATION RECORD

	Medication Name	Purpose	Color and Shape	Expiration Date	Imprint On Pill	Taken With or Without
1						
2						
3						
4						
5						

Introduction: Getting Started

Common Conditions

Common Conditions II

Relieving Aches & Pains

Chronic Conditions

Medical Consumerism

Getting Active

Managing Weight

Introduction:
Getting Started

Common
Conditions

Common
Conditions II

Relieving
Aches & Pains

Chronic
Conditions

Medical
Consumerism

Getting
Active

Managing
Weight

Imported Medications And Online Pharmacies

The rising costs of prescription drugs and the proliferation of online pharmacies bring about new challenges for healthcare consumers. Are imported medications safe? Are online pharmacies a good choice when looking for cost savings and convenience?

The Facts On Imported Medications

Simply stated, medications imported from outside the United States are illegal and not safe unless imported directly by the manufacturer of the drug under the supervision of the FDA. Imported drugs are not regulated by the FDA, and may be too strong or too weak—in either case, causing potential problems. Stay away from imported drugs.

The Facts On Online Pharmacies

Provided an online pharmacy is licensed by the National Association of Boards of Pharmacy (NABP), and you've discussed purchasing drugs online with your healthcare provider, online pharmacies may be an acceptable alternative to traditional pharmacies. However, online pharmacies are not right for everyone. Consider these points before purchasing from an online pharmacy.

✓ Online pharmacists cannot monitor blood pressure or cholesterol or help you remain compliant with your drug therapy.

✓ You may not have access to a pharmacist to answer your questions in a timely fashion.

✓ You won't be able to develop a strong relationship with your pharmacist in the manner you would if you visited a traditional pharmacist.

Ultimately, whether or not to purchase medications from an online pharmacy is an important decision you'll need to make very carefully and with the help of your healthcare team.

Medication Inventory (What To Have On Hand)

It is important to be prepared and have medications on hand for the unexpected. The following OTC medications will come in handy in your home.

▶ **Pain relievers**—Aspirin, acetaminophen, and ibuprofen for fevers, general aches and pains, and headaches. Do not give aspirin to children.

▶ **Cough syrup**—For common, mild coughs.

▶ **Antacids**—For indigestion, heartburn, and digestive discomfort.

▶ **Antihistamines**—For allergy symptom relief and sinus clearing.

▶ **Decongestants**—For sinus clearing.

▶ **Eye drops**—For sore, dry, red, and itchy eyes.

▶ **Triple antibiotic ointment**—Neosporin or similar product for infections, scrapes, cuts, punctures, and piercings.

▶ **Aloe Vera rub**—For burns, sunburns, scrapes, cuts, and punctures.

and How Much To Take	Doctor's Name and Phone #	Side Effects

Preventing **Medical Errors**

Introduction: Getting Started

Common Conditions

Common Conditions II

Relieving Aches & Pains

Chronic Conditions

Medical Consumerism

Getting Active

Managing Weight

Top Ten Tips

Even with skilled healthcare providers and advanced medical technology, unfortunately, medical errors still happen from time to time.

The good news is that medical errors can be prevented. The following tips are presented to help you take an active role in staying safe in the medical care system. Remember, as a consumer of medical care, much of the burden for preventing medical errors falls in your hands.

1 **Take an active role in your healthcare.** Sure, some mistakes happen because the healthcare system is complex, but many others happen because doctors and patients don't communicate clearly with each other. Taking an active role in your healthcare is the single most important thing you can do to prevent medical errors.

2 **Choose a hospital that has experience in the procedure you need.** Research shows that patients tend to have better results when they are treated at hospitals that have a great deal of experience with their condition.

3 **Make sure your healthcare provider knows about all medications you are taking.** Problems related to the use of pharmaceutical drugs account for nearly 10 percent of all hospital admissions. That's why it's a good idea at each annual check-up to bring in every medication you're taking (even over-the-counter medications) so your healthcare provider can update your files, and review potential complications.

4 **Double check your prescriptions, and then check them again.** According to the Institute of Medicine, as many as 7,000 deaths occur each year as a result of incorrect prescriptions. Check the label on your medicine bottle against the name on your prescription! Also, read the label directions carefully before leaving the pharmacy. Does "four doses daily" mean one pill every six hours around the clock, or just during waking hours?

5 **Understand your course of treatment.** When being discharged after a hospital procedure, ask your healthcare provider to explain your treatment plan. Healthcare providers often

"If you're going in for major surgery or an extended stay, have an advocate with you to help with critical decisions."

think they give more information than they really do, and to make things worse, a recent study showed that patients forget as much as 80 percent of what they are told by their healthcare provider within a short amount of time. Two key points here: 1.) Ask as many questions as you need to in order to feel comfortable, and 2.) Don't forget to write down instructions!

6 **Get an advocate.** If you're going in for major surgery or an extended stay, have an advocate with you to help with critical decisions—you may not be thinking clearly because of medications you're taking. Ask a family member or trusted friend to help get things done, and speak for your best interests when you can't.

7 **Ask healthcare workers to wash their hands.** Hand washing is an important way to prevent the spread of infections in hospitals. Yet, it is not done regularly or thoroughly enough. A recent study found that when patients checked whether healthcare workers washed their hands, the workers washed their hands more often and used more soap.

8 **Inform your doctor about any allergies you may have.** It doesn't matter how minor the allergy is, the healthcare provider still needs to know about it. Some people are allergic to certain antibiotics (like penicillin). It's especially important to inform your healthcare provider of this type of allergy in order to avoid potentially serious complications.

9 **Ask about tests and procedures.** Don't assume that no news is good news. By being informed, and asking about the outcomes of tests and procedures, you'll engage your healthcare provider in conversation that forces both of you to think through solutions, avoiding oversights and mistakes.

10 **Designate a lead care giver.** Make sure that a single healthcare provider (like your personal doctor) is in charge of your care instead of a group of caregivers who each know relatively little about your condition.

Source: Agency for Healthcare Research and Quality

Introduction: Getting Started

Common Conditions

Common Conditions II

Relieving Aches & Pains

Chronic Conditions

Medical Consumerism

Getting Active

Managing Weight

Introduction: Getting Started

Common Conditions

Common Conditions II

Relieving Aches & Pains

Chronic Conditions

Medical Consumerism

Managing Weight

About **Health Risk Appraisals**

Get A Handle On Your Health

Quantifying your health status is one of the single most important steps you can take in leading a long and healthy life. But, before you can work to improve your health status, you need to understand where you're starting from right now—that's why developing a keen understanding of your health status is so important.

Our health—good or bad—isn't a matter of luck. Rather, our health depends greatly on the lifestyle choices we make on a daily basis. How often we exercise, the types of food we eat, and whether or not we choose to drink or use tobacco, all have a major impact on our health and quality of life.

How we live accounts for more than half of the reasons we get sick or how we die. In fact, according to The Journal of the American Medical Association:

✓ Today's four leading causes of death are all preventable—smoking, poor nutrition, physical inactivity, and high-risk alcohol use.

✓ Persons with healthier lifestyles live anywhere from six to nine years longer than those with unhealthy lifestyles.

✓ Persons with healthier lifestyles not only live longer, but also prevent disability by up to nine years and shorten it at the end of their lives.

This means that the choices we make every day, have a powerful effect on not only how long we live, but also on the quality our lives.

Understanding HRAs

Quantifying your health status is a matter of assessing your current health behaviors, and identifying possible risk factors for disease and other health conditions you may have. One of the most important tools at your disposal for measuring health status and taking control of your own health is a health risk appraisal, or HRA.

A health risk appraisal is a short, confidential survey designed to assess your true health status. It's important to note, however, that unlike your personal healthcare provider, a health risk appraisal cannot diagnose illnesses or identify specific health problems. It can, however, provide an accurate picture of the lifestyle behaviors increasing your risk for different diseases or health conditions that may reduce the length and quality of your life.

The typical HRA starts with a confidential questionnaire (either paper or online) about your health and lifestyle habits (i.e. blood pressure, weight, tobacco use, physical activity, etc). After completing the questionnaire (which should take anywhere from 15 to 30 minutes), your

"One of the most important tools at your disposal for **measuring health status** and **taking control of your own health** is a health risk appraisal."

answers are then entered into a computer program, which analyzes your responses and creates a confidential profile that identifies your major health risks, and highlights healthy habits and changes you can make to reduce your health risks.

HRAs are an important part of taking responsibility for your own health, and becoming a wise healthcare consumer. Completing a health risk appraisal allows you to better understand your health risks, and formulate a plan for taking charge of your health in the years to come.

Questions To Expect

Although each HRA is unique, most will ask questions about the following topics.

- ✓ Blood pressure
- ✓ Weight status
- ✓ Tobacco use
- ✓ Sleeping habits
- ✓ Family health history
- ✓ Cholesterol
- ✓ Level of physical activity
- ✓ Alcohol use
- ✓ Stress
- ✓ Nutritional/eating habits

Family Medical History

Many HRAs will include questions about family medical history. Some health conditions tend to be hereditary, which may increase the risk that family members will experience the same health problems. The following list of conditions are thought to be hereditary in nature.

- ✓ Obesity
- ✓ Diabetes
- ✓ Heart disease
- ✓ Depression
- ✓ Gum disease
- ✓ Asthma
- ✓ Alcoholism
- ✓ High cholesterol
- ✓ Some cancers
- ✓ Glaucoma
- ✓ High blood pressure
- ✓ Sickle-cell anemia

Knowing your family health history can potentially help you avoid serious medical conditions to which you may be predisposed. Talk with your healthcare provider to evaluate your risks as they relate to family medical history.

Take Advantage

A variety of health risk appraisals are available to help you take control of your own health and well-being. And in many cases, your employer may even provide you with an opportunity to participate in a health risk appraisal free of charge. If this is the case, be sure to take advantage of the opportunity provided to you by your employer—it's one of the most important steps you can take to protect your health, and lead a long and healthy life.

▸ *A good health risk appraisal will ask straightforward questions about exercise habits, nutrition, stress, and tobacco use to evaluate your overall health and help you identify areas in need of improvement.*

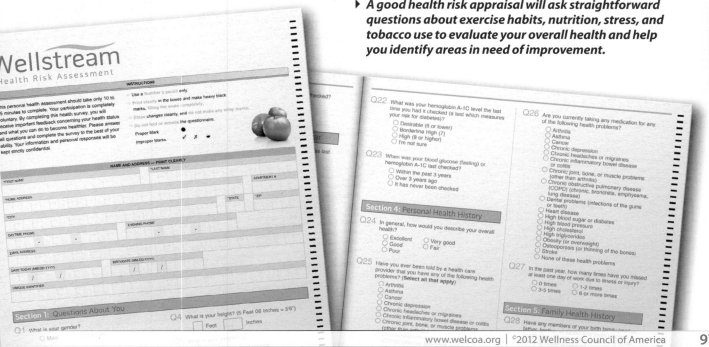

WHAT DO YOU KNOW ABOUT...

Medical Consumerism?

Take The Self-Care Quiz

The quiz below is designed to test your knowledge on the information presented in this section. Use this quiz as a tool to better understand how to care for yourself and others.

True   *False*

❏ ❏ **1)** Patients forget 80 percent of what a healthcare provider tells them as soon as they leave the office.

❏ ❏ **2)** Medical screenings should be performed only when a serious health problem is discovered.

❏ ❏ **3)** It's OK to take medication not prescribed for you, as long it comes from a family member.

❏ ❏ **4)** Avoiding medical errors is an important part of being a wise healthcare consumer.

❏ ❏ **5)** Many of today's leading causes of death are preventable.

Answers can be found inside this section.

Sidebar tabs:
Introduction: Getting Started
Common Conditions
Common Conditions II
Relieving Aches & Pains
Chronic Conditions
Medical Consumerism
Getting Active
Managing Weight

A Guide To
Getting Active

Understanding Physical Activity ★ Physical Activity & Your Heart ★ The Benefits & The Risks
Five Myths About Exercise ★ Before Starting ★ Preparing To Exercise
Exercise For Gain, Not Pain ★ Working Out Is Right For You

Self-Care **ESSENTIALS**®
A SIMPLE GUIDE TO MANAGING YOUR HEALTH CARE AND LIVING WELL

All About **Physical Activity**

Introduction: Getting Started

Common Conditions

Common Conditions II

Relieving Aches & Pains

Chronic Conditions

Medical Consumerism

Getting Active

Managing Weight

Is Exercise From Daily Activities Enough?

Most Americans get little vigorous exercise at work or during leisure hours. Today, only a few jobs require vigorous physical activity. People usually ride in cars or buses and watch TV during their free time rather than be physically active. Activities like golfing and bowling provide people with some benefit. But they do not provide the same benefits as regular, more vigorous exercise.

Evidence suggests that even low- to moderate-intensity activities can have both short- and long-term benefits. If done daily, they help lower your risk of heart disease. Such activities include pleasure walking, stair climbing, gardening, yardwork, moderate to heavy housework, dancing and home exercise. More vigorous exercise can help improve fitness of the heart and lungs, which can provide even more consistent benefits for lowering heart disease risk.

Today, many people are rediscovering the benefits of regular, vigorous exercise—activities like swimming, brisk walking, running, or jumping rope. These kinds of activities are sometimes called "aerobic"—meaning the body uses oxygen to produce the energy needed for the activity. Aerobic exercises can condition your heart and lungs if performed at the proper intensity for at least 30 minutes, 3-4 times a week.

But you don't have to train like a marathon runner to become more physically fit! Any activity that gets you moving around, even it it's done for just a few minutes each day, is better than none at all. For inactive people, the trick is to get started. One great way is to take a walk for 10-15 minutes during your lunch break. Other ideas in this section will help you get moving and living a more active life.

What Are The Benefits of Regular Physical Activity?

These are the benefits often experienced by people who get regular physical activity.

Feeling Better
Regular physical activity

✓ gives you more energy

✓ helps in coping with stress

✓ improves your self-image

✓ increases resistance to fatigue

✓ helps counter anxiety and depression

✓ helps you to relax and feel less tense

✓ improves the ability to fall asleep quickly and sleep well

✓ provides an easy way to share an activity with friends or family and an opportunity to meet new friends

Looking Better
Regular physical activity

✓ tones your muscles

✓ burns off calories to help lose extra pounds or helps you stay at your desirable weight

✓ helps control your appetite

Working Better
Regular physical activity

✓ helps you to be more productive at work

✓ increases your capacity for physical work

✓ builds stamina for other physical activities

✓ increases muscle strength

✓ helps your heart and lungs work more efficiently

Feeling, looking, and working better—all these benefits from regular physical activity can help you enjoy your life more fully.

How Much Physical Activity Is Needed To Lose Weight?

You need to burn off 3,500 calories more than you take in to lose one pound. If you want to lose weight, regular physical activity can help you in either of two ways.

First, you can eat your usual amount of calories, but be more active. For example: A 200-pound person who keeps on eating the same amount of calories, but decides to walk briskly each day for 1½ miles will lose about 14 pounds in one year. Or second, you can eat fewer calories and be more active. This is an even better way to lose weight.

The average calories spent per hour by a 150-pound person are listed below. (A lighter person burns fewer calories; a heavier person burns more.) Since exact calorie figures are not available for most activities, the figures below are averaged from several sources and show the relative vigor of the activities.

The calories spent in a particular activity vary in proportion to one's body weight. For example, a 100-pound person burns ⅓ fewer calories, so you would multiply the number of calories by 0.7. For a 200-pound person, multiply by 1.3.

Working harder or faster for a given activity will only slightly increase the calories spent. A better way to burn up more calories is to increase the time spent on your activity.

Activity	Calories Burned
>> Bicycling 6 mph	240 cals./hr.
>> Bicycling 12 mph	410 cals./hr.
>> Cross-country skiing	700 cals./hr.
>> Jogging 5 ½ mph	740 cals./hr.
>> Jogging 7 mph	920 cals./hr.
>> Jumping rope	750 cals./hr.
>> Running in place	650 cals./hr.
>> Running 10 mph	1280 cals./hr.
>> Swimming 25 yds/min.	275 cals./hr.
>> Swimming 50 yds/min.	500 cals./hr.
>> Tennis-singles	400 cals./hr.
>> Walking 2 mph	240 cals./hr.
>> Walking 3 mph	320 cals./hr.
>> Walking 4 ½ mph	440 cals./hr.

Introduction: Getting Started

Common Conditions

Common Conditions II

Relieving Aches & Pains

Chronic Conditions

Medical Consumerism

Getting Active

Managing Weight

Physical Activity & **Your Heart**

Introduction: Getting Started

Common Conditions

Common Conditions II

Relieving Aches & Pains

Chronic Conditions

Medical Consumerism

Getting Active

Managing Weight

The Benefits of A Well-Conditioned Heart

In one minute with 45 to 50 beats, the heart of a well-conditioned person pumps the same amount of blood as an inactive person's heart pumps in 70 to 75 beats. Compared to the well-conditioned heart, the average heart pumps up to 36,000 more times per day, 13 million more times per year.

Can Physical Activity Reduce My Chances of Having A Heart Attack?

Yes! Various studies have shown that physical inactivity is a risk factor for heart disease. Overall, the results show heart disease is almost twice as likely to develop in inactive people than in those who are more active. Regular physical activity (even mild to moderate exercise) can help reduce your risk of heart disease. In fact, burning calories through physical activity may help you lose weight or stay at your desirable weight—which also helps lower your risk of heart disease. The best exercises to strengthen your heart and lungs are the aerobic ones like brisk walking, jogging, cycling and swimming.

Coronary artery disease is the major cause of heart disease and heart attack in America. It develops when fatty deposits build up on the inner walls of the blood vessels feeding the heart (coronary arteries). Eventually one or more of the major coronary arteries may become blocked—either by the buildup of deposits or by a blood clot forming in the artery's narrowed passageway. The result is a heart attack.

We know that there are several factors that can increase your risk for developing coronary artery disease—and thus the chances for a heart attack. Fortunately, many of these risk factors can be reduced or eliminated.

"In one minute with 45 to 50 beats, the heart of a **well-conditioned person** pumps the same amount of blood as an **inactive person's** heart pumps in 70 to 75 beats."

Introduction:
Getting Started

Common
Conditions

Common
Conditions II

Relieving
Aches & Pains

Chronic
Conditions

Medical
Consumerism

**Getting
Active**

Managing
Weight

Heart Disease Risk Factors That You Can Do Something About

Cigarette Smoking, High Blood Pressure, High Blood Cholesterol, Physical Inactivity and Obesity. The more risk factors you have, the greater your risk for heart disease and heart attack.

✓ **Cigarette Smoking.** Heavy smokers are two to four times more likely to have a heart attack than nonsmokers. The heart attack death rate among all smokers is 70 percent greater than among nonsmokers. People who are active regularly are more likely to cut down or stop cigarette smoking.

✓ **High Blood Pressure.** The higher your blood pressure, the greater your risk of developing heart disease or stroke. A blood pressure of 140/90 mmHg (millimeters of mercury) or greater is generally classified as high blood pressure. Regular physical activity, even of moderate intensity, can help reduce high blood pressure in some people. This type of activity may also help prevent high blood pressure.

✓ **High Blood Cholesterol.** A blood cholesterol level of 240 mg/dL (milligrams per deciliter) or above is high and increases your risk of heart disease. A total blood cholesterol of under 200 mg/dL is desirable and usually puts you at a lower risk of heart disease. Cholesterol in the blood is transported by different types of particles. One of these particles is a protein called high density lipoprotein or HDL. HDL has been called "good" cholesterol because research has shown that high levels of HDL are linked with a lower risk of coronary artery disease. Regular moderate-to-vigorous physical activity is linked with increased HDL levels.

✓ **Physical Inactivity.** The lack of physical activity increases your risk for developing heart disease. Even persons who have had a heart attack can increase their chances of survival if they change their habits to include regular physical activity. It can help control blood lipids, diabetes and obesity as well as help to lower blood pressure. Also, physical activity of the right intensity, frequency and duration can increase the fitness of your heart and lungs— which may help protect you against heart disease even if you have other risk factors.

✓ **Obesity.** Excess weight may increase your risk of developing high blood pressure, high blood cholesterol and diabetes. Regular physical activity can help you maintain your desirable body weight. People at their desirable weight are less likely to develop diabetes. And, exercise may also decrease a diabetic person's need for insulin.

Remember that even if you are active, you should not ignore other risk factors. Reduce or eliminate any risk factors you can to lower your chances of having a heart attack.

Heart Healthy Tips

♥ Stay physically active.

♥ Stop smoking and avoid other people's smoke if possible.

♥ Control high blood pressure and high blood cholesterol.

♥ Cut down on total fats, saturated fats, cholesterol and salt in your diet.

♥ Reduce weight if overweight.

The Benefits & **The Risks**

Are There Risks In Exercising?

Muscles And Joints

One of the most common risks in exercising is injury to the muscles and joints. This usually happens from exercising too hard or for too long—particularly if a person has been inactive for some time. However, most of these injuries can be prevented or easily treated if you follow the tips found on pages 110 and 111.

Heat Exhaustion And Heat Stroke

If precautions are not taken during hot, humid days, heat exhaustion or heat stroke can occur—although they are fairly rare. Heat stroke is the more serious of the two. Their symptoms are similar:

Heat Exhaustion Risks

>> Dizziness
>> Headache
>> Nausea
>> Confusion
>> Body Temperature below normal

Heat Stroke Risks

>> Dizziness
>> Headache
>> Nausea
>> Thirst
>> Muscle Cramps
>> Sweating Stops
>> High Body Temperature

The last two symptoms of heat stroke are important to know. If the body temperature becomes dangerously high, it can be a serious problem.

Both heat exhaustion and heat stroke can be avoided if you drink enough liquids to replace those lost during exercise.

Heart Problems

In some cases, people have died while exercising. Most of these deaths are caused by overexertion in people who already had heart conditions. In people under age 30, these heart conditions are usually congenital heart defects (heart defects present at birth). In people over age 40, the heart condition is usually coronary artery disease (the buildup of deposits of fats in the heart's blood vessels). Many of these deaths have been preceded by warning signs such as chest pain, lightheartedness, fainting and extreme breathlessness. These are symptoms that should not be ignored and should be brought to the attention of a doctor immediately.

Some of the deaths that occur during exercise are not caused by the physical effort itself. Death can occur at any time and during any kind of activity—even eating and sleeping. This does not necessarily mean that a particular activity caused the death—only that the two events happened at the same time.

Introduction: Getting Started

Common Conditions

Common Conditions II

Relieving Aches & Pains

Chronic Conditions

Medical Consumerism

Getting Active

Managing Weight

No research studies have shown that physically active people are more likely to have sudden, fatal heart attacks than inactive people. In fact, a number of studies have shown a reduced risk of sudden death for people who are physically active.

Exercising too hard is not beneficial for anyone, however, it is especially strenuous for out-of-shape, middle-aged and older persons. It is very important for these people to follow a gradual and sound exercise program.

If you consider the time your body may have been out of shape, it is only natural that it will take time to get it back into good condition. A gradual approach will help you maximize your benefits and minimize your risks.

What If I've Had A Heart Attack?

Regular, brisk physical activity can help reduce your risk of having another heart attack. People who include regular physical activity in their lives after a heart attack improve their chances of survival. Regular exercise can also improve the quality of your life—how you feel and look. It can help you do more than before without pain (angina) or shortness of breath.

If you've had a heart attack, consult your doctor to be sure you are following a safe and effective exercise program. Your doctor's guidance is very important because it could help prevent heart pain and further damage from overexertion.

Benefits vs. Risks

Should you begin a regular exercise program? Consider the ways physical activity can benefit you and weigh them against the possible risks.

Potential Benefits

✓ more energy and capacity for work and leisure activities

✓ greater resistance to stress, anxiety and fatigue, and a better outlook on life

✓ increased stamina, strength and flexibility

✓ improved efficiency of the heart and lungs

✓ loss of extra pounds or body fat

✓ help in staying at desirable weight

✓ reduced risk of heart attack

Potential Risks

✓ muscle or joint injuries

✓ heat exhaustion or heat stroke on hot days (rare)

✓ aggravation of existing or hidden heart problems

"One of the **most common risks in exercising** is injury to the muscles and joints."

Introduction: Getting Started

Common Conditions

Common Conditions II

Relieving Aches & Pains

Chronic Conditions

Medical Consumerism

Getting Active

Managing Weight

Five Myths **About Exercise**

Myth 1:
Exercising Makes You Tired.
As they become more physically fit, most people feel physical activity gives them even more energy than before. Regular, moderate-to-brisk exercise can also help you reduce fatigue and manage stress.

Myth 2:
Exercising Takes Too Much Time.
It only takes a few minutes a day to become more physically active. To condition your heart and lungs, regular exercise does not have to take more than about 30 to 60 minutes, three or four times a week. If you don't have 30 minutes in your schedule for an exercise break, try to find two 15-minute periods or even three 10-minute periods. Once you discover how much you enjoy these exercise breaks, you may want to make them a habit! Then physical activity becomes a natural part of your life.

Myth 3:
All Exercises Give You The Same Benefits.
All physical activities can give you enjoyment. Low-intensity activities—if performed daily—also can have some long-term health benefits and lower your risk of heart disease. But only regular, brisk and sustained exercises such as brisk walking, jogging or swimming improve the efficiency of your heart and lungs and burn off substantial extra calories. Other activities may give you other benefits such as increased flexibility or muscle strength, depending on the type of activity.

Myth 4:
The Older You Are, The Less Exercise You Need.
We tend to become less active with age, and therefore need to make sure we are getting enough physical activity. In general, middle-aged and older people benefit from regular physical activity just as young people do. Age need not be a limitation. In fact, regular physical activity in older persons increases their capacity to perform activities of daily living. What is important, no matter what your age, is tailoring the activity program to your own fitness level.

Myth 5:
You Have To Be Athletic To Exercise.
Most physical activities do not require any special athletic skills. In fact, many people who found school sports difficult have discovered that these other activities are easy to do and enjoy. A perfect example is walking—an activity that requires no special talent, athletic ability or equipment.

106

Before **Starting**

Exercise Do's And Dont's...

Getting started with a regular exercise program is one of the best decisions you can make for your life. But before you jump right in, there are a few things you should know. Exercising safely is extremely important—without a firm grasp on the basics of staying safe, you could become injured, cutting short your quest to get in shape.

In the following pages, we'll cover the basics of safe exercise. From proper stretching techniques, to starting slowly, you'll learn what to look for (and what to look out for) when beginning a regular exercise routine. By paying attention to a few important details, you'll be well on your way to achieving your fitness goals and living a longer, healthier life—without getting injured along the way.

Before You Start An Exercise Program...

Most people do not need to see a doctor before they start since a gradual, sensible exercise program will have minimal health risks. However, some people should seek medical advice.

Use the following checklist to find out if you should consult a doctor before you start or significantly increase your physical activity.* Mark those items that apply to you:

☐ Your doctor said you have a heart condition and recommended only medically-supervised physical activity.

☐ During or right after you exercise, you frequently have pains or pressure in the left or mid-chest area, left neck, shoulder or arm.

☐ You have developed chest pain within the last month.

☐ You tend to lose consciousness or fall over due to dizziness.

☐ You feel extremely breathless after mild exertion.

☐ Your doctor recommended you take medicine for your blood pressure or a heart condition.

☐ Your doctor said you have bone or joint problems that could be made worse by the proposed physical activity.

☐ You have a medical condition or other physical reason not mentioned here which might need special attention in an exercise program. (For example, insulin-dependent diabetes.)

☐ You are middle-aged or older, have not been physically active, and plan a relatively vigorous exercise program.

If you've checked one or more items, see your doctor before you start. If you've checked no items, you can start on a gradual, sensible program of increased activity tailored to your needs. If you feel any of the physical symptoms listed above when you start your exercise program, contact your doctor right away.

*This checklist has been developed from several sources, particularly the Physical Activity Readiness Questionnaire, British Columbia Ministry of Health, Department of National Health and Welfare, Canada (revised 1992).

Introduction: Getting Started

Common Conditions

Common Conditions II

Relieving Aches & Pains

Chronic Conditions

Medical Consumerism

Getting Active

Managing Weight

Preparing To **Exercise**

Introduction: Getting Started

Common Conditions

Common Conditions II

Relieving Aches & Pains

Chronic Conditions

Medical Consumerism

Getting Active

Managing Weight

Five Steps For Success

Making physical activity a part of your daily life isn't an easy undertaking. It takes dedication, will power, patience, and a lot of hard work. But believe it or not, it's not as hard as it may first appear, and you might even be surprised to find that you enjoy your newfound lifestyle and the benefits it offers. But before we jump right in we'll want to look at five steps that will help you stay safe, have fun, and be successful at getting fit. Let's take a look at these five rules.

Step #1—Talk With Your Doc.

It's important to talk with your healthcare provider to identify whether your plans for physical activity are safe and right for you (see Checklist on page 107). Factors to consider include your blood pressure, past health problems, and current health conditions like diabetes or arthritis. All of these factors can have an impact on your exercise routine, and your health. Talking with your doc can help you identify issues that could harm or injure you while exercising, as well as help you put together a plan to work around those issues safely.

Step #2—Identify Your Barriers.

Beginning an exercise routine, especially if you've never been all that physically active, may seem a little frightening at first. So, by identifying barriers, you can confront them head on and prevent them from getting in your way. Common barriers include a fear of discomfort, a lack of time, or risk of injury. Begin by examining what barriers have prevented you from being physically active in the past, and find ways to address them. Ask questions like, "Do I really not have time to exercise, or am I just not making time for exercise?"

Step #3—Choose Your Weapon.

Identify what you're going to do to get physically active. Are you going to join a gym, start by walking, take on a new sport, or sign up for an aerobics or other fitness class? Start by taking an inventory of the things you like to do or maybe the things you're good at. If you're of the mindset that you only run when being chased, choosing an activity like jogging probably isn't going to help you get and stay active. You'll also want to give some consideration to any special equipment or clothing you may need for the activity of your choice. The proper gear may not only make your activity more enjoyable, but also, in some cases, help protect you from injury or discomfort.

Step #4—Set Your Goals.

Goals are actually one of the most important parts of your plan to get physically active. In many ways, they provide the roadmap for your success. Basically, you can't get to where you want, if you don't know where you're going. Begin by identifying what you want to accomplish by getting active. Maybe you want to lose 33 pounds, or maybe you want to fit into your favorite swimming suit by summer. Write down your goals and make them public. Doing so can help keep you motivated as you set out on your journey. Also, try setting mini goals that lead towards your main goal. If you want to lose 30 pounds in four months, set a goal of losing 8 pounds per month. And lastly, reward yourself each time you accomplish one of your goals—especially the big ones.

Step #5—Get Motivated.

Motivation will be a key factor in your success towards getting fit. Because exercising—at least at first—can be a little uncomfortable, it can be hard to stay motivated. Always keep in mind why you started exercising to begin with. What goals did you set? Keep in mind the benefits of your exercise program versus the consequences of giving up. Also, try to find someone who will support you or—even better—exercise with you. Having someone to keep you on track when you feel like loafing may just make the difference between success and starting over next year.

Play It Safe: Start Slowly & Build

There's probably nothing that can spoil your plans for getting physically fit faster, or more painfully, than getting injured. When beginning any new activity, the most important thing to remember is to start slowly and build. Taking on too much, too fast dramatically increases the chances that you'll get hurt in your quest to get well. Injury is a major reason many people never successfully reach their fitness goals. Starting slowly and building is the best way to play it safe, and perform better at your chosen activity.

Also, keep the following recommendations in mind as you begin your exercise routine.

1. **Learn and understand the inherent risk of the activity you're taking part in.** What muscles are you more likely to pull, or what other ways could you be injured?

2. **Use the recommended safety gear for your activity.** Walking or jogging in the wrong shoes could be just as dangerous as playing ice hockey without a helmet.

3. **Learn the proper technique for what you're doing.** While learning to walk properly is probably easier than learning to golf, understanding the basics involved in your activity will not only help you perform better, but also minimize the chances that you get injured.

4. **Always, always, always, listen to your body.** No matter how strenuous or mild your chosen activity is, you should never experience pain! Pain is a sign that something is wrong and that you need to stop!

"**Starting slowly and building is the best way** to play it safe, and perform better at your chosen activity."

Introduction: Getting Started

Common Conditions

Common Conditions II

Relieving Aches & Pains

Chronic Conditions

Medical Consumerism

Getting Active

Managing Weight

Introduction: Getting Started

Common Conditions

Common Conditions II

Relieving Aches & Pains

Chronic Conditions

Medical Consumerism

Getting Active

Managing Weight

Exercise For Gain, **Not Pain**

Stretching

If your idea of stretching is to reach across the table for another chicken wing, think again. Stretching is a great way for everyone to prevent aches and pains and can also help prevent injuries from overuse and repetitive motions, which account for one-third of all missed workdays. So what do you need to know about stretching? Remember the four basics—how to start, how to stretch, how often, and how long.

How Do I Start?

Warming up can help your stretching results. A light warm-up before stretching can help increase your range of motion, but will not prevent injury. Try jumping jacks or walking in place to get the muscles active and warm.

How Should I Stretch?

Slow and controlled—not fast—and avoid bouncing. Also, it's best to hold the stretch continuously for 15 to 30 seconds per muscle group. If you feel any pain, back off. Pain is your body's way of telling you that you have gone beyond your limits.

How Often?

One stretch per muscle group, once a day should be sufficient. However, some muscle groups may require more stretching.

How Long?

For 15 to 30 seconds per muscle group. Research shows that this is effective for both immediate and long-term results.

These recommendations are for healthy individuals. If you are injured or have other health conditions, be sure to consult your physician before starting a routine.

Source: Physicians and Sportsmedicine

Six Tips For Safe Exercise

Are you a "weekend warrior?" Do you try to push yourself during exercise or sports even when you know you shouldn't? If you answered, "yes" to these questions, you're a prime candidate for an exercise injury. In addition to following the central recommendations in this section, keep the following six quick tips in mind to stay even safer when exercising.

1 | **Get good advice.** Consulting a professional— like a personal trainer—on how to use equipment and build your ability will help you improve your skills and exercise safely. Often, an initial consultation is free of charge.

2 | **Wear proper clothing.** Lightweight, breathable clothing is important when exercising indoors or in high heat/humidity. Remember to wear several layers when exercising in cold temperatures. Also, try to stay comfortable—tight clothing can cause irritation and chaffing.

3 | **Get equipped.** Safety equipment—whether you like the way it looks or not—can go a long way in helping you prevent injury. Helmets are especially important if engaging in outside activities like bicycling or rollerblading.

4 | **Don't make the same mistake twice.** Injuries are often the result of overuse—running too fast or too far, too soon. If you get injured or experience discomfort, don't just "work through it" blindly. Determine how it happened and correct the problem.

5 | **Get plenty of rest.** Exercising before an old injury has time to fully heal can lead to another injury. If you're still in pain, or the injury site is still inflamed, don't exercise.

6 | **Continually educate yourself.** Even after you're in great shape, and you've worked through most of your questions, it's still a good idea to try to learn more about exercising properly. A variety of great websites and books are available to help keep you in the know.

Introduction: Getting Started

Common Conditions

Common Conditions II

Relieving Aches & Pains

Chronic Conditions

Medical Consumerism

Getting Active

Managing Weight

Introduction: Getting Started

Common Conditions

Common Conditions II

Relieving Aches & Pains

Chronic Conditions

Medical Consumerism

Getting Active

Managing Weight

Working Out Is **Right For You**

Activate Yourself!

As mentioned throughout this section, exercising is one of the most important steps you can take to leading a long and healthy life. Regular physical activity has been shown to reduce your risk for heart disease, help you control your weight, lower your cholesterol levels, improve your blood pressure, reduce stress and increase energy. But you have to exercise the right way to obtain these benefits.

Health experts generally agree that adults should engage in "moderate-intensity" physical activity for at least 30 minutes on five or more days of the week. But what is "moderate intensity," and how can you be sure you're working out at a level that will provide long-term health benefits? Read on to get answers to these important questions.

Getting In The Zone

Understanding how certain activities rate on the intensity scale is only the beginning when it comes to getting a good workout. To truly get health benefits, train aerobically, lose weight, and derive long-term health benefits, you'll need to "get in the zone,"—in the target heart rate zone that is.

Determining your target heart rate is a fairly easy process. The simplest way to do it is to subtract your age from 220. This will give you your maximum heart rate (the maximum number of times your heart can safely beat in one minute).

Once you have determined your maximum heart rate, you'll want to exercise with enough intensity to keep your heart rate between 60 and 70% of your maximum heart rate. After approximately six months of regular exercise, you can safely exercise up to about 85% of your maximum heart rate.

Check out the example target heart rate calculation below to get a better look at calculating your target heart rate.

Calculating Target Heart Rate

(Example for a 45 year old individual)

220 minus age (45) = 175 beats per minute
(maximum heart rate)

60-70% of 175 = 105-123 beats per minute

85% of 175 = 149 beats per minute

By exercising between 60 and 85% of your maximum heart rate, you'll increase your cardiovascular fitness, lose weight, and derive long-term health benefits.

Introduction:
Getting Started

Common
Conditions

Common
Conditions II

Relieving
Aches & Pains

Chronic
Conditions

Medical
Consumerism

**Getting
Active**

Managing
Weight

Target Heart Rate Made Easy!

Using A Heart Rate Monitor

These days, determining your heart rate while exercising is a snap—get a heart rate monitor (HRM). A heart rate monitor is a simple strap that fits snugly around your chest that measures your heart rate and transmits the data to a device worn like a wristwatch.

Available at almost all sports equipment stores, basic heart rate monitors ($50-$75) will accurately tell you your heart rate and record information on your exercise session. Some more expensive models can provide other information like:

✓ Number of calories burned in a workout

✓ Average heart rate over entire exercise period

✓ Fat calories burned

✓ Time "in the zone"

Using a heart rate monitor eliminates the guesswork most people have about their workouts, and the benefits are huge. You'll know that each workout is an investment in your future.

Take The Test

If you don't feel like wearing a heart rate monitor or calculating beats per minute, there's a simple test you can do while exercising to determine the intensity of your workout. It's called the "talk test."

The talk test method of measuring intensity is simple. If you're exercising at a light intensity level you should be able to sing while doing the activity. If you're exercising at a moderate intensity level you should be able to carry on a conversation comfortably while engaging in the activity. Finally, if you become winded, or too out of breath to carry on a conversation, you're exercising at a vigorous intensity level.

Try the talk test. It's tried and true, and has helped many exercisers maximize their workouts.

A Matter of Feel

The third method of determining physical activity intensity is a method called the Borg Rating of Perceived Exertion (RPE). While it may sound complicated, RPE is simply a measure of how hard you feel like your body is working. It is based on the physical sensations you experience during physical activity—things like a higher heart rate, breathing harder, or sweating more.

Although this is a subjective measure, experts agree that RPE provides a fairly good estimate of the actual heart rate during physical activity. The RPE scale starts at six (classified as "no exertion" whatsoever) and goes up to 20 (called "maximal exertion"). To keep your exercise at a moderate level, shoot for a workout that feels like you're at 12-14 on the scale.

Obviously, you'll get better at ranking your workout as you exercise more, but give RPE a try—without a heart rate monitor, or a workout buddy to talk to, it may be your best bet to measure workout intensity.

WHAT YOU SHOULD KNOW ABOUT...

Getting Active.

Working Out Is Right For You

Exercise may very well be the magic bullet. It's important to get off on the right foot. Check out the following before getting started.

✓ **Talk to your healthcare provider.** If it's been a long time since you last got any physical activity, be sure to talk with your doctor about the best way to begin your exercise program.

✓ **Choose activities that are right for you.** Choosing an activity you like will help you stick with it.

✓ **Be comfortable.** Make sure your clothing and shoes encourage exercise, not hamper it.

✓ **Find a friend.** Having someone to exercise with is more fun than going it alone. It also increases the chances that you'll exercise more.

✓ **Don't overdo it.** If it's been a while, start with lighter intensity activities and build from there.

The information found on pages 100-107 of this section was gathered from a publication developed by the American Heart Association (AHA) and the National Heart, Lung, and Blood Institute (NHLBI). This information was originally developed by the NHLBI (NIH 81-1677) and has been adapted and reprinted by the American Heart Association for use in public education and community service programs. The information is in the public domain and may be used and reprinted without permission.

The information found on pages 108-114 was taken from WELCOA's line of Physical Activity brochures. All information has been reviewed for accuracy. This information is not intended to replace the advice of your healthcare provider. If you have any questions about managing your own health and/or seeking medical care, please contact a medical professional.

Introduction:
Getting Started

Common
Conditions

Common
Conditions II

Relieving
Aches & Pains

Chronic
Conditions

Medical
Consumerism

Getting
Active

Managing
Weight

A Guide To
Managing Weight

Understanding Your Weight ★ Assessing Your Weight Status ★ Choosing The Right Foods
Understanding Portion Size ★ Getting Your Five-A-Day ★ Recognizing Fad Diets

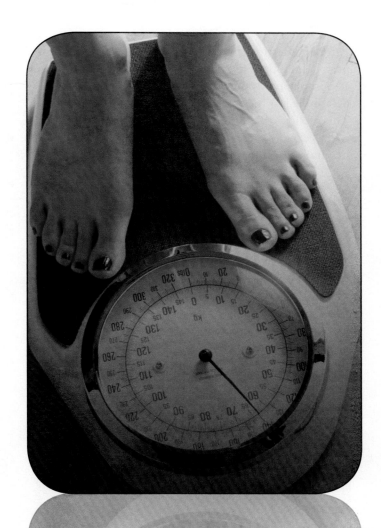

Self-Care ESSENTIALS®
A SIMPLE GUIDE TO MANAGING YOUR HEALTH CARE AND LIVING WELL

Sidebar navigation (left margin):
Introduction: Getting Started
Common Conditions
Common Conditions II
Relieving Aches & Pains
Chronic Conditions
Medical Consumerism
Getting Active
Managing Weight

Understanding **Your Weight**

Thinking About Weight

According to several health experts, overweight and obesity has become the number one health problem in the United States today. The majority of Americans are either overweight or obese (extremely heavy), and the end appears to be nowhere in sight. Making the issue even more critical, obesity claims approximately 300,000 lives each year, second only to cigarette smoking.

Part of addressing this escalating health issue is taking personal responsibility for your own weight. The first step is to honestly and accurately assess your weight to determine just how many pounds you may need to lose. This section will outline ways to assess your weight as well as explore some simple strategies to help you maintain a healthy weight.

Did You Know?

✓ A weight loss of five to 10 percent in excess body weight can significantly reduce risk factors and provide health benefits

✓ Overweight and obesity are associated with heart disease, certain types of cancer, type 2 diabetes, stroke, arthritis, breathing problems, and psychological disorders such as depression

✓ Obesity-related costs in the U.S. total approximately $100 billion annually

✓ Americans spend an estimated $33 billion each year on weight loss products and services

✓ Each year, an estimated 300,000 U.S. adults die of causes attributable to obesity

✓ Type 2 diabetes is nearly 3-4 times more prevalent in overweight adults than in lean adults

✓ Men who are more than 20 percent overweight have a 20-30 percent increase in death from prostate cancer

✓ The percentage of children and adolescents who are defined as overweight has more than doubled since the early 1970s

Source: Surgeon General, CDC, and Dr. Donnica.com

"Part of addressing this escalating health issue is **taking personal responsibility for your own weight.**"

Why Are We Gaining So Much Weight?

Certainly, there are several contributing factors for why Americans are gaining so much weight—a problem so widespread is bound to be pretty complicated. But after all is said and done, experts agree on at least three key factors driving overweight and obesity in the U.S. today. They are outlined below.

Factor #1: The Working Life

The world of work is changing. Cell phones, pagers, faxes, and e-mails now dominate our working lives. And while Americans aren't working any less, they are moving less. One hundred years ago, most people made their living through hard physical work—farming the land, building railroads, and burning calories. Today, more than half of us sit in front of a computer all day, burning very few calories at all. Even those of us not using computers during the day are burning fewer calories because of technological advancements that make our work easier.

Factor #2: Food, Food, Food

Food is abundantly available—in fact, it's everywhere. And America is eating it up. Americans now spend more money on fast food than on higher education, personal computers, computer software, or new cars. They spend more on fast food than on movies, books, magazines, newspapers, videos, and recorded music—combined. Consider this: In 1970, Americans spent about $6 billion on fast food; in 2000, they spent more than $110 billion.

Factor #3: Our Sedentary Society

In total, there are 168 hours in every week. The vast majority—nearly 70%—are devoted to sedentary activities. Consider that employed adults work an average of 47 hours per week. In addition, the typical American spends 16 hours and 55 minutes sitting in front of the TV, and averages 50.6 hours of sleep. These three everyday activities alone account for over 113 sedentary hours per week—almost five days of not moving!

Sources: Fast Food Nation, The Overworked American, and The National Sleep Foundation

Shedding Pounds The Right Way

Listed here you'll find three key things to keep in mind when attempting to lose weight—they will be referenced throughout this section. Don't forget to check with your healthcare provider before making important changes, and remember to take it slow. Getting hurt is no fun, and it will set you back in reaching your goals.

1. Adjust Your Diet.

A few simple changes can make a big difference when it comes to what you eat. Because one pound of fat is equal to 3,500 calories, cutting just a few hundred calories out of your diet each day can go a long way. Easy ways to cut calories include eating less dressing and sauce and substituting an apple or banana for your afternoon candy bar.

2. Increase Physical Activity.

We're not talking about running a marathon here—in fact, that's the last thing you want to do if you're just getting started. Begin to increase physical activity by making small changes like parking your car farther away from the entrance of a store or taking the stairs instead of the elevator. Later, you may want to start taking short walks in the evening hours after work.

3. Avoid Fad Diets.

Stay away from fad diets at all costs. Why? Plain and simple, they just don't work. The only way to lose weight and keep it off is to adjust what you eat and get more activity into your daily routine.

Introduction: Getting Started

Common Conditions

Common Conditions II

Relieving Aches & Pains

Chronic Conditions

Medical Consumerism

Getting Active

Managing Weight

Assessing **Your Weight Status**

Introduction: Getting Started

Common Conditions

Common Conditions II

Relieving Aches & Pains

Chronic Conditions

Medical Consumerism

Getting Active

Managing Weight

The Right Weight

One of the most important steps people can take to protect their health is becoming aware of their true weight status. Our weight, be it healthy or not, can be an important risk factor for a number of diseases such as heart disease, cancer, and diabetes. In fact, more than 300,000 Americans die each year from diseases caused or worsened by overweight and obesity. So, it's important to know your true weight status.

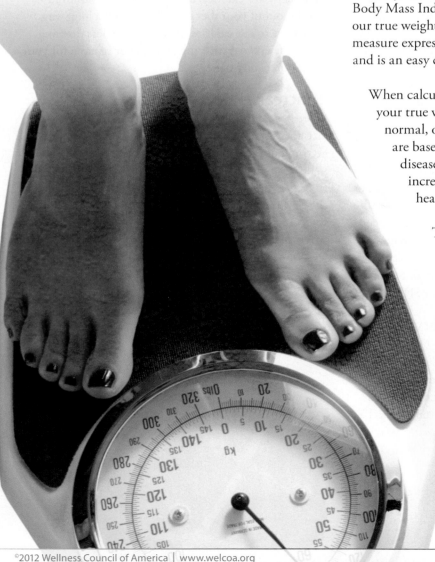

You're probably wondering, "How can I determine my true weight status?" Unfortunately, because we tend to underestimate our weight, and overestimate our health, we need some help. The best way to measure our weight status is, "by the numbers." This means using a tool like Body Mass Index (BMI). Don't worry, it's not as scary as it sounds, and understanding BMI could be one of the most important things to know about your health. The rest of this section will help you understand a little bit more about this tool for determining your weight status.

Body Mass Index

Body Mass Index (BMI), is one of the best measures of our true weight status. Put simply, BMI is a common measure expressing the relationship of weight-to-height, and is an easy calculation using inches and pounds.

When calculated, your BMI will help you determine your true weight status as either underweight, normal, overweight, or obese. These BMI ranges are based on the effect of weight status on disease and death. Generally, as a person's BMI increases, so does their risk for a number of health conditions and diseases.

These include the risk of premature death, heart disease, high blood pressure, osteoarthritis, cancer, and diabetes.

"**Our weight,** be it healthy or not, **can be an important risk factor for a number of diseases** such as heart disease, cancer, and diabetes."

Calculating Your BMI

The BMI Chart found below *(Chart 2)* makes determining your BMI easy. Simply find your height and weight and circle the number where the two lines intersect. This is your BMI. Once you have determined your BMI, you can use this number to determine weight status (using *Chart 1*—underweight, normal, overweight, or obese). BMI values for adults are interpreted using a fixed number, regardless of age or sex, using the following guidelines:

Chart 1

BMI	Weight Status
Below 18.5	Underweight
18.5 - 24.9	Normal
25.0 - 29.9	Overweight
30.0 and above	Obese

Using *Chart 1*, we can tell that a BMI of 25.0 is defined as being overweight. As *Chart 2* shows, as BMI increases, your risk for disease increases as well.

"Body Mass Index **(BMI),** **is one of the best measures** *of our true weight status."*

Chart 2

Body Mass Index Table

	Normal						Overweight					Obese										Extreme Obesity														
BMI	19	20	21	22	23	24	25	26	27	28	29	30	31	32	33	34	35	36	37	38	39	40	41	42	43	44	45	46	47	48	49	50	51	52	53	54
Height (inches)																	Body Weight (pounds)																			
58	91	96	100	105	110	115	119	124	129	134	138	143	148	153	158	162	167	172	177	181	186	191	196	201	205	210	215	220	224	229	234	239	244	248	253	258
59	94	99	104	109	114	119	124	128	133	138	143	148	153	158	163	168	173	178	183	188	193	198	203	208	212	217	222	227	232	237	242	247	252	257	262	267
60	97	102	107	112	118	123	128	133	138	143	148	153	158	163	168	174	179	184	189	194	199	204	209	215	220	225	230	235	240	245	250	255	261	266	271	276
61	100	106	111	116	122	127	132	137	143	148	153	158	164	169	174	180	185	190	195	201	206	211	217	222	227	232	238	243	248	254	259	264	269	275	280	285
62	104	109	115	120	126	131	136	142	147	153	158	164	169	175	180	186	191	196	202	207	213	218	224	229	235	240	246	251	256	262	267	273	278	284	289	295
63	107	113	118	124	130	135	141	146	152	158	163	169	175	180	186	191	197	203	208	214	220	225	231	237	242	248	254	259	265	270	278	282	287	293	299	304
64	110	116	122	128	134	140	145	151	157	163	169	174	180	186	192	197	204	209	215	221	227	232	238	244	250	256	262	267	273	279	285	291	296	302	308	314
65	114	120	126	132	138	144	150	156	162	168	174	180	186	192	198	204	210	216	222	228	234	240	246	252	258	264	270	276	282	288	294	300	306	312	318	324
66	118	124	130	136	142	148	155	161	167	173	179	186	192	198	204	210	216	223	229	235	241	247	253	260	266	272	278	284	291	297	303	309	315	322	328	334
67	121	127	134	140	146	153	159	166	172	178	185	191	198	204	211	217	223	230	236	242	249	255	261	268	274	280	287	293	299	306	312	319	325	331	338	344
68	125	131	138	144	151	158	164	171	177	184	190	197	203	210	216	223	230	236	243	249	256	262	269	276	282	289	295	302	308	315	322	328	335	341	348	354
69	128	135	142	149	155	162	169	176	182	189	196	203	209	216	223	230	236	243	250	257	263	270	277	284	291	297	304	311	318	324	331	338	345	351	358	365
70	132	139	146	153	160	167	174	181	188	195	202	209	216	222	229	236	243	250	257	264	271	278	285	292	299	306	313	320	327	334	341	348	355	362	369	376
71	136	143	150	157	165	172	179	186	193	200	208	215	222	229	236	243	250	257	265	272	279	286	293	301	308	315	322	329	338	343	351	358	365	372	379	386
72	140	147	154	162	169	177	184	191	199	206	213	221	228	235	242	250	258	265	272	279	287	294	302	309	316	324	331	338	346	353	361	368	375	383	390	397
73	144	151	159	166	174	182	189	197	204	212	219	227	235	242	250	257	265	272	280	288	295	302	310	318	325	333	340	348	355	363	371	378	386	393	401	408
74	148	155	163	171	179	186	194	202	210	218	225	233	241	249	256	264	272	280	287	295	303	311	319	326	334	342	350	358	365	373	381	389	396	404	412	420
75	152	160	168	176	184	192	200	208	216	224	232	240	248	256	264	272	279	287	295	303	311	319	327	335	343	351	359	367	375	383	391	399	407	415	423	431
76	156	164	172	180	189	197	205	213	221	230	238	246	254	263	271	279	287	295	304	312	320	328	336	344	353	361	369	377	385	394	402	410	418	426	435	443

Source: Adapted from Clinical Guidelines on the Identification, Evaluation, and Treatment of Overweight and Obesity in Adults: The Evidence Report.
http://www.nhlbi.nih.gov/guidelines/obesity/bmi_tbl.pdf

Introduction: Getting Started

Common Conditions

Common Conditions II

Relieving Aches & Pains

Chronic Conditions

Medical Consumerism

Getting Active

Managing Weight

Choosing **The Right Foods**

The Mediterranean Diet: 50 Essential Foods

Recently, the "Mediterranean Diet" has received increased attention as a healthy way to reduce weight and maintain excellent health and body weight over the course of your lifetime. The term "Mediterranean Diet" refers to the traditional diet consumed by people who live around the Mediterranean Sea. And while foods consumed in that part of the world often differ from country to country, the common thread is a plant-based diet low in meat and moderate in fat—with much of the fat coming from olive oil. Numerous studies attest to the health benefits of this diet and prove that traditional Mediterranean foods are ideal for long-term weight management.

The following list comes from Mary Flynn, PhD, expert on the Mediterranean Diet and author of *Low Fat Lies, High Fat Frauds, And The Healthiest Diet In The World*. Flynn suggests stocking up on the following items and making them a regular part of your diet. Doing so will help you manage your weight and live a long, healthy life—all the while enjoying what you eat!

1. Anchovy fillets or paste

2. Artichokes—canned or jarred

3. Asparagus—canned or frozen

4. Beans—canned (such as cannellini, red beans, and chickpeas)

5. Bread—pita or high-fiber

6. Breakfast cereal—especially high fiber, minimum five grams per serving (such as Shredded Wheat, All Bran, Fiber One, Grape Nuts, and oatmeal)

7. Broccoli—frozen

8. Canola Oil

9. Capers

10. Carrots—fresh

11. Cheese—like swiss, provolone (nothing wrong with the occasional piece, but don't overdo it—you want to stay away from saturated fat), also grated parmesan or romano, part-skim mozzarella

12. Chicken/beef broth—canned or bouillon cubes

13. Chicken breasts

14. Canned clams

15. Eggs

16. Feta cheese—crumbled

17. Fruits—canned (such as peaches and pears packed in juice, not syrup)

Introduction: Getting Started

Common Conditions

Common Conditions II

Relieving Aches & Pains

Chronic Conditions

Medical Consumerism

Getting Active

Managing Weight

18. Garlic cloves

19. Grape juice—purple (especially if you can't drink alcohol or red wine)

20. Green/Red peppers—fresh

21. Ham—lean and sliced (use only occasionally)

22. Herbs and spices (such as salt, red pepper flakes, black pepper, fresh or dried basil, oregano, parsley, and rosemary)

23. Fresh Lemons

24. Lentils—dry

25. Lentil soup—canned

26. Milk—nonfat

27. Mushrooms—fresh and canned

28. Olive oil—preferably extra virgin

29. Olives—canned and packed in brine (sliced, whole)

30. Onions—red and white

31. Pasta—short noodles like ziti for easy measuring, preferably high-fiber, four grams of fiber per serving (for a good-tasting, high-fiber pasta, try Delverde whole-wheat pasta)

32. Peas—canned or frozen

33. Pine nuts (pignolis)

34. Potatoes—fresh

35. Raisins

36. Red wine—one-half glass to one glass with dinner (omit if there is a health reason preventing you from drinking wine)

37. Rice—preferably brown (brown rice is higher in fiber and more nutritious)

38. Roasted red peppers—jarred

39. Shrimp—frozen

40. Spinach/Kale—frozen

41. Tomatoes—canned and paste

42. Tomatoes—fresh (in season)

43. Tuna—canned in water

44. Turkey—sliced (occasional use of meat is okay, but avoid ground beef)

45. Various fresh fruits in season (such as grapes, figs, tangerines, plums, oranges, strawberries, apples, etc.)—three times a day

46. Various fresh vegetables in season (such as arugula, eggplant, spinach, broccoli, broccoli rabe, kale, asparagus, cucumbers, etc.)

47. Vegetable medleys—frozen

48. Vinegar—basalmic

49. Walnuts and other nuts—shelled

50. Yogurt—plain

Introduction: Getting Started

Common Conditions

Common Conditions II

Relieving Aches & Pains

Chronic Conditions

Medical Consumerism

Getting Active

Managing Weight

Understanding **Portion Size**

Portion Your Platter

You don't have to stop eating all your favorite foods in order to eat healthy. In fact, you can still enjoy ice cream or occasional fast food, as long as you control your portions and are physically active on most days of the week. Remember, like most things in life, the key to eating healthy is moderation.

So how much is too much? Well, serving sizes are designed to help you determine how much to eat at meals so you won't over-indulge on some of your favorites. Check out the suggestions listed here to help you judge if you're eating the right serving sizes. With the help of some visual aids, eating the right amounts won't be such a challenge.

How Much Is That?

The following comparisons will help you estimate the right amount of food to eat in one sitting.

✓ Three ounces of meat is about the size of a single deck of cards

✓ One serving of meat, fish, or poultry is about the size of a computer mouse

✓ One-half cup of cut fruit or vegetables, pasta, or rice is about the size of a small fist

✓ One cup of milk, yogurt, or chopped fresh greens is about the size of a tennis ball

✓ One ounce of snack food (e.g., pretzels, chips) is about one large handful

✓ Three ounces of grilled fish is about the size of your checkbook

✓ One ounce of cheese is about the size of four dice

   ✓ Two tablespoons of peanut butter is about the size of a ping pong ball

      ✓ An average-sized bagel is about the size of a hockey puck (about half the size of the gigantic bagels we're used to!)

"You don't have to stop eating all your favorite foods in order to eat healthy."

Sidebar tabs: Introduction: Getting Started | Common Conditions | Common Conditions II | Relieving Aches & Pains | Chronic Conditions | Medical Consumerism | Getting Active | Managing Weight

"Plain and simple, **in the battle to cut portion size, fruits and vegetables will help you feel full and save on calories** at the same time."

Introduction:
Getting Started

Common
Conditions

Common
Conditions II

Relieving
Aches & Pains

Chronic
Conditions

Medical
Consumerism

Getting
Active

Managing
Weight

Eating Out: Tips For Eating Smaller Portions

Try the following tips the next time you visit your favorite restaurant—they'll help you control your portion sizes.

✓ **Order a chicken sandwich.** Try ordering a grilled chicken sandwich the next time you visit a fast food restaurant. By substituting a grilled chicken sandwich for a cheeseburger with the works, you'll save about 150 calories.

✓ **Order the small fries.** By eating only a small order of fries instead of the "super-sized" fries, you'll save about 300 calories.

✓ **Don't drown yourself in soda.** A small soda has 150 fewer calories than a large one.

✓ **Share and share alike.** This is simple math. If you share an entrée with a friend the next time you visit a restaurant, you'll only eat half as much.

✓ **Order an appetizer.** But only an appetizer! Getting an appetizer instead of a main course can help control the amount you eat because appetizers are often much smaller than entrées.

✓ **Get it to-go.** Ask for half your meal to be packaged in a "to-go" box, and eat it for lunch the next day.

Staying At Home: Tips for Eating Smaller Portions

OK, so those are some tips for eating out, what about reducing portion sizes when eating at home? Check out the following tips.

✓ **Don't "bag it."** If you're snacking at home, put a few pretzels or chips in a small bowl instead of eating by the handful right out of the bag.

✓ **Go single.** Instead of buying snack foods in bulk (or even by the box) buy single servings—this way you won't eat the whole box/bag in a moment of weakness.

✓ **Take half off.** When using butter, sour cream, mayonnaise and cheese, use only half the amount you usually do. It may take some getting used to, but it's easier than going without. Also, check out some of the low-fat varieties of these spreads, they can be very good. Remember: Just because it's low fat or low calorie, doesn't mean you can eat as much as you want. Calories add up, even when you're eating low-calories or low-fat food.

Still Hungry?

Cutting portion sizes takes some getting used to. If, after attempting to cut your portion size, you're still feeling hungry, try filling up on fruits and vegetables. The American Cancer Society recommends five or more servings of fruits and vegetables each day to help prevent cancer, and chances are you're not getting enough. By filling up on fruits and vegetables, you'll not only cut your cancer risk but you'll also be substituting low-calorie, high-fiber food for higher calorie foods and snacks. Plain and simple, in the battle to cut portion size, fruits and vegetables will help you feel full and save on calories at the same time. Give 'em a try!

Source: American Cancer Society

Getting Your **Five-A-Day**

Introduction:
Getting Started

Common
Conditions

Common
Conditions II

Relieving
Aches & Pains

Chronic
Conditions

Medical
Consumerism

Getting
Active

**Managing
Weight**

The Power of Fruits & Vegetables

Only one in five Americans eats the recommended five to nine servings of fruits and vegetables each day.

But, what would you think if someone told you that consuming the daily-recommended number of fruits and vegetables could dramatically reduce your risk for serious diseases like heart disease or cancer? Would you doubt it? If so, you may just be surprised by the amazing preventive power of fruits and vegetables.

Getting Your Five In Three Easy Steps

By now we know that eating five to nine servings of fruits and veggies every day isn't easy. Our lives are extremely busy, and sometimes just finding enough time to eat is difficult—let alone finding time to eat the recommended amount of fruits and vegetables.

But have no fear—there's no reason to get down about our diets. Below you'll find three strategies that will help you eat great throughout the day, no matter where you are, what your budget is like, or how much time you have. Let's take a look.

Step #1: Incorporate Fruits & Vegetables Into Every Meal.

If you think about it, fruits and veggies are actually some of the fastest and simplest foods to eat and cook with. Below you'll find some ideas on how to fit fruits and vegetables into your daily eating routine.

▶ **Breakfast**
Slice a banana or some strawberries on top of your usual bowl of cereal. You may also want to drink some fruit juice. As long as it's 100% juice, just six ounces counts as one serving toward your five-a-day.

▶ **Lunch**
Pack some carrot sticks or broccoli for dipping instead of those greasy potato chips. Not only will you get one of your five-a-day servings out of the way, but you'll cut fat and calories at the same time.

▶ **Dinner**
There's nothing like a baked potato as part of a healthy dinner—as long as you don't load it up with toppings that increase calories and fat. Also, cooking up a can of corn or green beans in the microwave is about as simple as it gets.

Step #2: Make Your Fruits & Veggies Work For You.

Depending on what you buy and when, fresh fruits and veggies can be expensive. But they don't have to be. Check out these tips for saving big when it comes to getting your five-a-day.

▶ **Be a Bargain Hunter**

When learning how to shop smart for fruits and vegetables, you'll need to learn your prices. Once you have a good idea of what constitutes a good deal, you'll be able to load up on your favorite items. Don't forget, it helps tremendously if you can buy produce that's in season and local. You won't pay extra to have it shipped.

▶ **Freeze!**

Once you learn to recognize a bargain when you see one, chances are you'll have too much produce to eat before it spoils. The solution? Just freeze it. There's nothing wrong with freezing fruit. It keeps very well and in some cases, can make fruit even easier to work with. Consider refrigerating bananas, the skins may darken, but they'll last a few days longer.

▶ **Let It Grow**

Looking for the ultimate money saving technique when it comes to getting your five-a-day? Grow a garden! Sure, there will be some expense wrapped up in seed, water, and fertilizer, but the cost will be quite low. Plus, there's nothing quite like the feeling of eating homegrown food. Eat healthy and start a new hobby all at once!

Continued on the following page...

"Consuming the daily-recommended number of fruits and vegetables **could dramatically reduce your risk for serious diseases** like heart disease or cancer"

Introduction: Getting Started

Common Conditions

Common Conditions II

Relieving Aches & Pains

Chronic Conditions

Medical Consumerism

Getting Active

Managing Weight

Getting Your **Five-A-Day**

Continued...

Step #3: Get Your Five On The Go.

There's no doubt that Americans are working harder, and spending more time at work than at any other point in history. But this is no excuse to eat poorly—in fact, quite the opposite is true. If we're going to maintain our work pace, we have to make sure we're getting the nutrition and energy we need. The fact is, you can get your five-a-day no matter where you are.

▶ Eating Away from Home

The key to getting your five-a-day—even when you're away from the house—is substituting. Just because your favorite restaurant has certain menu items, doesn't mean you have to stick to them. Try substituting fresh fruit for fries, or vegetables in place of potato chips.

▶ Eating in the Car

Americans are spending more and more time in their cars—either commuting to and from work, or racing around running errands. To eat healthier when you're out and about, try keeping some dried fruit in your glove compartment, or bring something easy like cauliflower or grapes to snack on in between stops.

▶ At Work

Most foods people consume at work come straight from the vending machine. And these foods, rather than being loaded with healthy vitamins and minerals, are packed with extra calories and loads of fat. The following tips can help you eat healthier when you're at the office.

✓ Bring fresh fruit for everyone at your next staff meeting, instead of bagels or donuts.

✓ Store dried fruits such as raisins in your desk. This way, there's no reason to hit the vending machine.

✓ Collect recipes for salads or other healthy dishes that are quick and easy to prepare.

"If we're going to maintain our work pace, we have to make sure we're getting the nutrition and energy we need. The fact is, **you can get your five-a-day no matter where you are.**"

Step #1: Incorporate Fruits & Vegetables Into Every Meal.

Step #2: Make Your Fruits & Veggies Work For You.

Step #3: Get Your Five On The Go.

Introduction: Getting Started

Common Conditions

Common Conditions II

Relieving Aches & Pains

Chronic Conditions

Medical Consumerism

Getting Active

Managing Weight

Recognizing **Fad Diets**

Introduction: Getting Started

Common Conditions

Common Conditions II

Relieving Aches & Pains

Chronic Conditions

Medical Consumerism

Getting Active

Managing Weight

Why Fad Diets Don't Work

The plain and simple fact about fad diets—regardless of what they promise—is this: THEY DON'T WORK. And not only are they ineffective, but some can also be very dangerous for you. But despite their danger, millions and millions of Americans are looking for "quick-fix" weight loss solutions.

There are many reasons fad diets are flawed, but they all share one thing in common. They don't encourage behavior change. Losing weight, and keeping it off for life requires you to make actual lifestyle changes. You have to develop good eating habits, and make physical activity a part of your life. And believe it or not, this isn't breaking news—the word "diet" actually comes from the Greek word "diaita," which means, "manner of living." Even the ancient Greeks understood that losing weight was a matter of making lifestyle changes.

Fad Diet Flaws

The following are common flaws shared by fad diets…

! First and foremost, fad diets do not encourage lifestyle changes—the central aspect of healthy, successful weight management.

! Fad diets violate the first principle of good nutrition—eat a balanced diet that includes a variety of healthy foods.

! Super foods don't exist. It's important to eat moderate amounts of food from all food groups, not large amounts from a few.

! Fad diets aren't enjoyable. They tend to be so bland and boring that most people can only hold out for a short period of time.

Read on to learn more about spotting fad diets, and what it takes to lose weight safely.

"There are many reasons **fad diets are flawed**, but they all share one thing in common. **They don't encourage behavior change.**"

Spotting Fad Diets

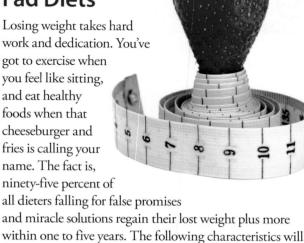

Losing weight takes hard work and dedication. You've got to exercise when you feel like sitting, and eat healthy foods when that cheeseburger and fries is calling your name. The fact is, ninety-five percent of all dieters falling for false promises and miracle solutions regain their lost weight plus more within one to five years. The following characteristics will help you spot a fad diet a mile away...

▶ **Miracle foods that burn fat.**
There are no such thing as "foods that burn fat." Healthy weight loss involves nutritious eating and increased physical activity.

▶ **Bizarre quantities.**
Look out for "miracle diets" that involve bizarre quantities of food. You're better off paying attention to the portion sizes of foods you normally eat. Oftentimes, portion sizes are twice what they should be for healthy eating.

▶ **Rigid menus.**
A healthy diet is a balanced diet. If you find a diet that rigidly restricts what you eat, take a closer look—it may be a fad diet.

▶ **Specific food combinations.**
As far as combinations are concerned, the two most important combinations involved with managing your weight are diet and exercise. Eat nutritiously and exercise more.

▶ **Rapid weight loss.**
Be aware of diets or programs that promise rapid weight loss. In a typical, healthy weight loss program, you shouldn't lose more than two pounds per week.

▶ **No physical activity involved.**
Managing and losing weight is a matter of calories in, calories out. To burn calories in a healthy way, you need to increase the amount of physical activity you're getting. When you find a diet that doesn't involve physical activity—it's not healthy.

The Usual Suspects: Five Popular Fad Diets

There are literally hundreds and hundreds of fad diets on the market today. In fact, the diet industry has become a booming business—Americans spend more than $33 billion per year on diet plans, equipment, and supplements. But Americans are still gaining weight. That's because fad diets, like the popular one's below, can't help you lose or maintain weight safely. Avoid these fad diets at all costs.

Suspect #1: The Food Specific Diet

Food specific diets are diets that require you to eat a specific food designed to encourage weight loss. These types of diets, especially if sustained over a long period of time, can deny your body important nutrients it needs to function properly.

Suspect #2: The High-Protein, Low-Carbohydrate Diet

The idea behind this fad diet is that cutting "carbs" will cut calories. And while this diet can be effective in cutting calories, it fails to acknowledge the important role carbohydrates play in providing your body the energy it needs for an active life.

Suspect #3: The High-Fiber, Low-Calorie Diet

Although fiber is an important part of a healthy diet, and can play an important role in weight loss, this diet typically encourages the consumption of unusually high levels of fiber, which can cause diarrhea, bloating, and cramping.

Suspect #4: The Liquid Diet

Although liquid diets can produce short-term weight loss, they fail in a major way because they do not encourage any behavior change. Liquid diets can very often be too low in calories, which will eventually inhibit your body's ability to lose weight.

Suspect #5: The Fasting Diet

Fasting actually slows your body's ability to lose weight. When you fast, your body isn't getting the fuel it needs. Instinctively, your body begins storing fat and burning muscle, which slows your metabolism—making it harder to lose weight.

WHAT YOU SHOULD KNOW ABOUT...

Managing Weight.

Introduction: Getting Started

Common Conditions

Common Conditions II

Relieving Aches & Pains

Chronic Conditions

Medical Consumerism

Getting Active

Managing Weight

Nutrition Fast Facts

✓ The typical American now consumes three hamburgers and four orders of French fries every week.

✓ 30% of adults eat out for lunch on the weekdays.

✓ Americans now spend more money on fast food than on higher education, personal computers, computer software, or new cars—COMBINED.

✓ The average business lunch is only 36 minutes long.

✓ In 1999, of the 30 fastest growing US franchises, 12 were fast food—and only three were fitness and nutrition.

✓ Nearly 10% of all food purchased in restaurants is consumed in the car.

✓ There are nearly 2 million different combinations of sandwiches that can be created from a Subway menu.

Source: Fast Food Nation